Never Too Young to Lead

Never Too Young to Lead

Developing Leadership in Young Adolescents

Maureen P. Provencher

Saint Mary's Press®

The publishing team included Laurie Delgatto, development editor; Lorraine Kilmartin, reviewer; prepress and manufacturing coordinated by the prepublication and production services departments of Saint Mary's Press.

Copyright © 2006 by Saint Mary's Press, Christian Brothers Publications, 702 Terrace Heights, Winona, MN 55987-1318, www.smp.org. All rights reserved. No part of this book may be reproduced by any means without the written permission of the publisher.

Printed in the United States of America

3821

ISBN 978-0-88489-873-3

Library of Congress Cataloging-in-Publication Data

Provencher, Maureen P.
  Never too young to lead : developing leadership in young adolescents / Maureen P. Provencher.
    p. cm.
  ISBN 978-0-88489-873-3 (pbk.)
   1. Church work with teenagers. 2. Church group work with teenagers. 3. Christian leadership. I. Title.
BV4447.P76 2006
259'.23—dc22
                                                              2005033256

Author Acknowledgments

I wish to thank the following people for their continued love, encouragement, support, and presence in my life: my family, the Adamses, the Gosselins (whose basement became a second home for me during this project), Marilyn, FM, JPL, and Lee.

Special thanks to my editor, Laurie Delgatto, for her inspiration and support.

Thanks to all the adults who see potential in so many young people, who nurture it and call it forth; who love them as they are, always aware of God's very presence within them. For the encouragement, support, mentoring, and love you freely offer in nurturing the seed of faith, thank you.

Thanks to Roland and Claire Boucher and all the adults in my young life who responded to the potential they saw in me. For you I am forever grateful.

Last, in thanksgiving to God for the privilege to have been led to many different communities of faith to minister to and with, and for some incredibly inspiring young people within whom the Holy Spirit is alive and well. To all of you, thank you for your willingness to allow God to shape your life and, in turn, shape our world through your action and presence. You truly have touched my life and those of many, many others.

Contents

Introduction 7

1 Leading as Jesus Did
    Ready to Begin: For the Sake of Others 11
    Ready to Be Formed: How Jesus Led 16
    Ready to Be Empowered: Called to Lead 20
    Prayer of Sending Forth 22

2 Listening as a Christian Leader
    Ready to Begin: Listening to Others 25
    Ready to Be Formed: Listening to God 29
    Ready to Be Empowered: A Way of Listening 32
    Prayer of Sending Forth 35

3 Conflict Resolution
    Ready to Begin: How We Approach Conflict 39
    Ready to Be Formed: Mediation 42
    Ready to Be Empowered: Forgiveness and Conflict 46
    Prayer of Sending Forth 50

4 Trust-Based Leadership
    Ready to Begin: Building Trust 57
    Ready to Be Formed: Becoming Trustworthy 61
    Ready to Be Empowered: Trust and Responsibility 64
    Prayer of Sending Forth 67

5 Leadership and Discipleship
    Ready to Begin: Models of Discipleship 69
    Ready to Be Formed: Servant Leadership 73
    Ready to Be Empowered: Discipleship Rooted in Christ . . 76
    Prayer of Sending Forth 80

6 Planning and Strategy
    Ready to Begin: Planning Skills 83
    Ready to Be Formed: Planning Skills in Practice 87
    Ready to Be Empowered: Implementing the Plan 90
    Prayer of Sending Forth 93

Acknowledgments 96

Introduction

Never Too Young to Lead: An Overview

Because younger adolescents make up an integral part of the Church, parish communities benefit from the zest offered by this particular age-group. Young people, as we know, question and challenge; they help us to dream and vision what can be; their idealism helps us to see with new eyes and consider the possibilities. They show us the ageless face of Christ, also reflected by them as they are—fearfully and wonderfully created.

Not only does our Church benefit from all the good this age-group has to offer, Christ himself depends on them, just as he depended on so many of the saints and people of the Bible. The experiences of faith that younger adolescents have to share, their gifts and talents, their enthusiasm and the individual uniqueness each of them has to offer are essential to the wholeness of our parish communities. Just as "the eye cannot say to the hand, 'I have no need of you,'" (1 Cor. 12:21), our communities need the participation of our young people. We are called to invite and include the participation of the young adolescents within our faith communities in the life and mission of Jesus, the mission of the Church, in which we all share. A commitment to forming our young people to Christian leadership connects to that very mission.

Never Too Young to Lead offers faith communities resources and strategies to develop leadership qualities and skills in young adolescents. The manual includes six themes on Christian leadership: leadership styles, listening skills, conflict resolution, trust and responsibility, leadership and discipleship, and planning and strategy. Each chapter contains three sessions to explore the themes; you will want to select the sessions that best meet the needs of your group. You may choose to use all the sessions in each chapter or you may choose to use just one. The sessions provide a broad overview of leadership with the aid of scriptural images, and include activities for training youth in essential leadership skills and qualities. The manual also offers strategies for using the sessions to create daylong, weekend, or weeklong training programs for young adolescents.

Three Stages of Readiness

Three separate sessions comprise each chapter of *Never Too Young to Lead*. The sessions are geared to address the needs of young people, accepting them "where they are at" through the use of three readiness stages: ready to begin, ready to be formed, and ready to be empowered. These stages are not based on chronological age or grade level; rather they are developed with the individual young person in mind.

> The **Ready to Begin** stage is intended primarily for younger adolescents who have had little or no leadership experience. This first stage introduces young adolescents to leadership, intentionally keeping the faith element light and inviting.

The **Ready to Be Formed** stage is intended primarily for young adolescents who have had some leadership experience, as well as those who have had some experience of service. Examples might include young teens who are new to altar serving, lecturing, music ministry, service programming, and student government, and those who display team sportsmanship. Overall these young people will have already displayed some leadership potential on which to build.

The **Ready to Be Empowered** stage is geared for young adolescents who are becoming "seasoned" in ministry through their involvement and activity, for example, those who have served as lectors; altar servers; cantors; class presidents, vice presidents, and other offices; team captains; those who grasp catechesis with enthusiasm; those who have been or currently are being mentored; those who have experience planning activities; and so on. These young people will have obvious leadership potential on which to build.

The sessions in each chapter can be utilized in whatever form or structure best fits the young people you gather. The chapters, as well as the three sessions within each chapter, are comprehensive and build on each other, though they can be used in any order, or they may be used as individual sessions that stand independently of one another.

Within each chapter is a brief overview of each session. In addition, the sessions include a checklist of required materials and preparation, followed by a complete description of the session procedure. The session is intended to fit a 60- to 90-minute time frame, with the exception of those noted as half-day sessions, and will vary depending on the size of the group you have gathered. Session components are as follows:

- **Gathering activity and introduction.** This activity invites the participants to gather, build community, and begin to focus on the session theme. The introduction provides the participants with a clear overview, or "taste," of what to expect from the session.
- **Learning activity and discussion.** In this segment the participants explore the theme in depth through the Scriptures, activities, and discussion. Ministry leaders present additional background and information to periodically augment the participants' work. It is from this segment that comparisons to real-life situations concerning the session's theme will be discussed and considered.
- **Prayer of sending forth.** Each chapter concludes with a prayer experience focused on the chapter's theme. The different kinds of prayer include guided meditation, shared prayer, music, reflective silence, prayer that is written and led by young people, and reflective reading. The prayer experience gives the young people an opportunity to offer their hearts and lives to God by presenting their insights and concerns to God in prayer. The time frame for prayer experiences varies from 5 to 20 minutes.

How and When to Use the Sessions

The following list offers a sampling of the variety of ways you might consider using the sessions in *Never Too Young to Lead* to create daylong, weekend, or weeklong training programs.

- Use the program within a catechetical structure for a six-week leadership training course. Select six sessions, one from each chapter, according to the readiness stage of the group you will be gathering.

- During the summer months, plan a summer leadership course, inviting the young people to gather once a week throughout July and August.
- Conduct one leadership session per month for the entire year.
- Where the stages of readiness within a group may vary, select a chapter and experience all three of its sessions together in progression.
- Conduct an overnight or two-day leadership retreat, using all the sessions in chapter 5 in sequential order. To add a service outreach component to the retreat, use all the sessions of chapter 4 in sequential order.
- To focus more on skill building, look to chapter 1, "Ready to Be Formed: How Jesus Led"; chapter 2, "Ready to Begin: Listening to Others"; chapter 3, "Ready to Be Empowered: Forgiveness and Conflict"; and chapter 6, "Ready to Begin: Planning Skills."
- To coordinate sessions offering off-site and active service outreach, look to chapter 1, "Ready to Be Empowered: Called to Lead"; chapter 4, "Ready to Be Empowered: Trust and Responsibility"; chapter 5, "Ready to Be Formed: Servant Leadership"; and chapter 6, "Planning and Strategy," in sequential order.
- For more reflective sessions, look to chapters 4 and 5.
- For more active sessions, look to chapter 2, "Ready to Begin: Listening to Others"; chapter 4, "Ready to Begin: Building Trust" and "Ready to Be Formed: Becoming Trustworthy."

Facilitating the Sessions

Role Models

Through the example of youth ministry leaders (both adults and youth), young people learn what it means to be a Christian leader. It is essential that those in positions of leadership be attentive to the example they are setting, in both words and actions. It is also important that they use, during the sessions and throughout the year, the leadership skills they are teaching.

Hospitality and Community Building

Hospitality and community building are significant parts of all youth ministry functions, including leadership team meetings and leadership training sessions. An important aspect of community building is the attitude of those involved in leadership. Leaders, both youth and adults, must build community with those who attend events and programs.

Presentations

In each session the leaders are asked to make presentations of key concepts and teachings. Ensure that those presentations are effective by practicing them ahead of time, personalizing the materials with the addition of your own stories and examples, familiarizing yourself with the material, and inviting constructive criticism from other leaders. If necessary, do some outside reading or learning about the ideas you will be presenting. The quality of the leadership training young people receive in these sessions will depend, in part, on how well you know the concepts yourself and how familiar you are with the material.

Facilitation

The skills of large-group facilitation are important. When working with the young people, the leaders of sessions or activities should have a strong understanding of the entire session and their role within it. The leaders should be attentive to the time allotted for each activity and to the core purpose of the activity.

Preparing Yourself

Read each session or activity before you facilitate it, and then use it creatively to meet the needs of the young people in your group. Some activities require preparation. Allow yourself adequate time to get ready.

Standard Materials

To save time, consider gathering frequently used materials into bins and storing those bins in a place accessible to all staff and volunteer leaders. Here are some recommendations for organizing a supply bin.

Supply Bin

The following items appear frequently in the materials checklists:
- masking tape
- cellophane tape
- nametags
- markers
- pens or pencils
- self-stick notes
- scissors
- newsprint
- unlined paper, scrap paper, or notebook paper
- index cards
- baskets
- candles and matches
- items to create a prayer space (for example, a colored cloth, a cross, a Bible, a bowl of water, and a vase for flowers)

1 Leading as Jesus Did
Ready to Begin: For the Sake of Others

Overview

Jesus did not use his energy to tear down, but to build up, to create and restore. How we use our energy directly affects our style of leadership. The choices we make and the example of how we live shape our world, whether it is good or bad. In this session the young people will explore how they use their energy, identifying what gives them energy and what robs them of their energy. In addition, they will be given the opportunity to consider how they are called to be creators, builders, and restorers—just like Jesus—through the use of their energy and gifts.

Preparation

- Gather the following items:
    - ☐ eight decks of regular playing cards
    - ☐ two buckets or baskets labeled "charity bank"
    - ☐ newsprint
    - ☐ Legos™, Lincoln Logs™, Tinker Toys™, Popsicle sticks, or other building materials at your disposal; enough supplies for every four participants to build a "house"
    - ☐ paper and markers
    - ☐ glue
    - ☐ several images of houses in need of restoration, taken from home-and-living–type magazines or downloaded photos from the Web; you will need one image for every four participants
- Separate all the jacks, queens, and kings from the decks of playing cards.
- Recruit two young people to serve as "charity bankers." Provide the bankers with all the jacks, queens, and kings from the deck of cards, telling them that whenever someone approaches them, they are to collect three cards from that individual and, in return, give that person a "trump card," that is, a jack, queen, or king.
- Recruit three young people to secretly be the "zippers." Provide each zipper with a deck of cards. You will also need to recruit three others to be the "zappers." Provide the zappers with five cards of low value. Then provide the following directions:
    - The zappers job is to mingle with the group, discreetly approaching people one at a time and "zapping" their energy by taking away two cards of your choice. Remember, the cards are worth their face value. Taking away two cards highest in value would be to your benefit.
    - Zippers, you have been given an entire deck of cards, and your job is to mingle as well; however, you are in the business of giving people energy. You

will do this by discreetly approaching people one at a time and giving each person two cards of a high value.
- The object for both the zappers and the zippers is to not be obvious to the others.
- But there's a catch for the zappers: if someone you approach happens to present you with a king, queen, or jack, you have automatically been transformed into a zipper.

1. Gather the group, and randomly distribute five playing cards to each participant. Then introduce the activity as follows:
- Each of you have been given five playing cards that hold their face value. For the sake of this game, these cards represent the level of energy you have.
- Among you, in this game, are zappers and zippers. Zappers are people who will "zap" you of your energy, symbolized by the playing cards. Whenever a zapper approaches you and asks you for your energy, you must allow him or her to take two of your cards.
- Then there are the zippers. Zippers are people who "zip" up your energy. Whenever a zipper approaches you, that person will give you two cards of her or his choice.
- You will not be able to tell a zipper from a zapper until you are approached by one.
- During the game, you will have a choice to either keep the cards you have or bank some in the "charity bank."
- Whenever you bank your cards, you will gain one certain benefit: a trump card. The trump cards are the kings, queens, and jacks. They are gained by banking a minimum of three of your cards at any time.
- It's important to note that a trump card will reverse the role of a zapper to a zipper! If a zapper approaches you and you have a trump card, that zapper becomes a zipper.
- Your goal as a player in this game is to not end up empty-handed. If you are getting low on energy (the number of cards you have in hand), you will want to seek out a zipper to gain more energy. Remember to beware of the zappers!

2. Check to see if there are any questions and, if so, respond and clarify as needed. Allow the game to go on for about 5 minutes. Be sure to pay close attention to the activity so as to be able to share what you observe.

3. Summarize the experience by inviting the participants to respond to some of the following questions, and by offering some of the following comments as well:
- Count up the face value of the cards you still hold. Who has 10 points, 20 points, 30 points (and so on)?
- For those with the fewest points, how did you use your energy during the game? For those with the most points, how did you use your energy? What were the risks you took? What did you gain?
- How many of you chose to keep as many of your cards as possible? What were the benefits and risks of keeping your energy to yourself? What kind of an effect will keeping your energy and gifts to yourself have on your friendships, family, teams, and clubs?

Then offer the following comments:
- The zappers represent the things and people in our lives who steal away, or "zap," our energy. Some of the things that zap our energy might include that we worry a lot and lose sleep over some things we can't change or control, or that someone in our lives is persistent in tempting us to consider trying something that would not be good for us, like drugs, for example.
- The zippers represent the things and people in our lives who boost, or "zip," our energy. Some of the things that zip our energy might include a simple kindness that was shown to us, like a smile or a hug; a compliment or a word of support; some time spent with God in prayer; or a person who believes in our abilities and encourages us.

4. Now tally up the value of the cards placed within the charity bank. Note how generous the group was or was not. Then discuss the following questions with the participants:
- How might this relate to sharing your energy positively with others?
- How might some of the injustices of our world, like homelessness, poverty, and hunger, be affected if we were to commit to giving to charity regularly through donations of time and money?

Then offer the following comment:
- The charity bank represents the times we share our gifts and energy with others, when we go beyond ourselves and meeting our own needs. And, as we know, there are benefits for ourselves to sharing what we have with others. It feels good to do something for others, and when love is shared, oftentimes it is returned a hundredfold. So it is with this game. When goodness is given freely, goodness grows.

5. Now ask the following questions. Be sure to record the answers on newsprint.
- What are some of the positive ways young people today use their energy?
- What are some of the negatives ways young people use their energy?

6. Make the following points in these or your own words:
- How we use our energy directly affects our style of leadership. Think of all the ways you use your energy: what you spend your time doing, what you spend your time thinking about, and how much time you spend worrying about what to say or what to wear, being kind to others, or perhaps at times gossiping about others.
- Based on how you use your energy, think about the leadership you model for others. If we look to Jesus as our ultimate model of leadership, we see time and time again that he always used his energy to glorify God and to benefit others. This is what true Christian leadership is all about.
- Jesus had tremendous energy, and he knew how and where to direct it. For example, he often refused to engage in meaningless conversation with people who wanted to argue rather than learn. He did not waste his time or energy even at his trial with what would have been a meaningless defense.
- Leadership is directly connected to the example of how we live and how we choose to use our energy. For example, other people watch what we do,

imitate us, follow our lead, can fall under our influence, and so on. Some other examples include:
- If we choose to seek to "get our way" all the time, our style of leadership will be very directive and we may not be open to what others have to share.
- If we choose to experiment with sex or drugs, our style of leadership is showing others irresponsibility and disrespect.
- If we take the time to listen to a friend who needs to talk, our style of leadership is one of compassion and understanding.
- If we choose to go to church every Sunday, our style of leadership shows that God is important in our lives.
- Each of us needs to be in tune with our source of energy. Like Jesus, we too must use our energy intentionally and purposefully.

7. Have the participants form two groups, assigning one group the role of "creators" and asking them to gather around the tables with the Legos, Lincoln Logs, Tinker Toys, paper, markers, glue, and Popsicle sticks, and any other materials that are available. Assign the second group the role of "restorers," asking them to gather around the tables with the images of houses already supplied for them. Within each group, ask the participants to pair off with a partner. Provide a sheet of newsprint and a few markers for each pair. Then explain that in this next exercise, they will be creating or renovating "houses."

Tell the creators that each pair is to create a house using the supplies provided. Tell the restorers that each pair's task is to develop plans to restore the house found in one of the photographs provided. Do not provide any further instructions except to inform them that they have only 10 minutes to complete the task.

8. Ask for a few volunteers to share their creations or restorations with the entire group, allowing 5 to 10 minutes for all who want to share. Keep the group seated at their respective tables and conclude the activity by sharing the following comments and questions:
- Take a moment to consider the way you used your energy in this activity. Were you more like an architect who dreams and can envision what the house can be? Were you like a builder who can take a plan and make it a reality by focusing on the pieces that fit together? Were you like a restorer who can take what is and make it beautiful and like new again?

9. Distribute a piece of paper and markers to each of the participants and ask them to draw the outline of a house. Provide these instructions:
- Consider situations that need to be recreated, built up, and restored, for example, a group of your peers at school who are constantly ridiculed or harassed or a sports team that needs some good motivation to work together. Take a quiet moment to write about or to draw symbols representing these situations.

10. Allow a few moments for the participants to accomplish this task. Have them write the following phrase at the bottom of their drawings:
- I am capable of creating, building, and restoring by how I use my energy.

Then offer the following comments:
- Jesus is the ultimate leader. He showed us how to lead by the way he lived.
- Jesus led by compassion and forgiveness, by choosing the right actions and by ultimate love.

- Jesus did not use his energy to tear down, but to build up, to create and restore. For example, he did not condemn the woman caught in adultery. Instead, he told her that her sins were forgiven and to go and sin no more (John 8:1–11). He did not ignore the blind man by just walking by him. Instead, he restored his sight (Mark 8:22–26).
- Jesus did not give up on the Apostles when they were in the midst of a storm at sea and his closest friends didn't trust that he would be able to keep them safe because he had fallen asleep! Instead, he challenged their faith a bit but calmed their fears (Luke 8:22–25).
- Being a Christian leader is all about becoming a creator, a builder, and a restorer. As Christian leaders we are challenged to share our ideas and energies freely and for the benefit of others.

Invite everyone to take their drawings home and to consider creating, building, or restoring just one of the situations during the coming week.

11. Conclude the session by leading the participants in the prayer service, "Prayer of Sending Forth," at the end of this chapter.

Ready to Be Formed: How Jesus Led

Overview

Being a leader does not always mean being the person in charge, or the only person with the responsibility. In simpler terms we can say that being a leader does not necessarily mean being "the boss." Being a leader means knowing when to lead and how to provide direction, consult others, and share responsibilities. In this session the young people will learn about three styles of leadership: directive, shared, and "let it be," as well as types of situations for which each of these styles is often best suited. In addition, the group will explore Scripture stories that portray the different styles of leadership Jesus used.

Preparation

- Gather the following items:
  - ☐ three tables
  - ☐ three shoe boxes
  - ☐ markers and paper
  - ☐ three pairs of scissors, three balls of yarn, three bottles of glitter, and three bottles of glue
  - ☐ various magazines
  - ☐ a red hat, a yellow hat, and a green hat; instead of hats, you may choose to have a red piece of yarn, a yellow piece, and a green piece worn as a visible necklace by selected team members or young people
  - ☐ a timer or stopwatch
  - ☐ newsprint
  - ☐ three copies of *The Catholic Youth Bible*® or another Bible
- Set up three tables. Place a set of glitter, glue, scissors, magazines, paper, markers, yarn, and one shoe box on each table.
- Select either three adult team members or three young people to wear a colored hat or necklace and role-play the various leadership styles, as assigned. Be sure to inform them that they are never to give away their roles, always staying true to their roles no matter what happens. The roles are as follows:
  + Red = the "directive" leader. This person will aggressively direct the group by telling them what to do for the task. The directive leader will limit discussions on suggestions and ideas and will deliberately not ask for the opinions of others.
  + Yellow = the "sharing" leader. This person will actively ask others for their ideas and opinions on how to perform the task. The sharing leader may provide some direction yet is always committed to creating a positive environment of teamwork in which everyone has a sense of ownership.
  + Green = the "let it be" leader. This person will intentionally give little or no direction to the group in accomplishing the task. The let-it-be leader will offer opinions only when asked by the group and will allow the leadership of others to come forth.

Leading as Jesus Did

1. Begin by separating the participants into three equal groups. Assign each group a table and ask the group members to be seated. Explain, using these or similar words:
  - Each group's task is to create a "show box" that displays the uniqueness and the commonalities of your group members.
  - You will do this by using the craft supplies that have been provided at each table.
  - The object is to present the most creative and well-displayed "show box."
  - But, there are three "managers" who are "in charge" and responsible for the tasks at hand. These managers can be identified by the red, yellow, and green hats or necklaces. They will be coming around to work with your groups for short periods of time.
  - Each of the managers will rotate into each of the three groups during the activity. Whenever the timer or stopwatch dings, the managers will move on to another group. Remember, they are responsible for your work on the task.

2. Check to see if anyone has questions and, if so, offer responses and clarification as needed. Then assign each one of the managers to a table. Remind the participants that every few minutes a new manager will be sent to their group. Set the timer for 3 minutes and then begin. When the timer goes off, remind the managers to move to the next table. Then reset the timer for three more minutes. Repeat these steps another time, allowing a total of about 9 or 10 minutes for the groups to create and prepare their show boxes. Take good mental or written notes of what you observe so you can share them later in the session.

3. Ask the three groups to present their show boxes and describe what their experiences were like when working with the different managers. Ask for specifics, and record them on newsprint.

4. Focus the groups' attention by introducing the three managers and their specific roles, explaining the three styles of leadership as follows:
- *The "directive" leader.* This person's role was to aggressively direct the group by telling them what to do for the task. The directive leader was to limit discussions on suggestions and ideas and to deliberately not ask for the opinions of others.
- *The "sharing" leader.* This person's role was to actively ask others for their ideas and opinions on how to perform the task. The sharing leader provided some direction yet was always committed to creating a positive environment of teamwork in which everyone had a sense of ownership.
- *The "let it be" leader.* This person's role was to intentionally give little or no direction to the group in accomplishing the task. The let-it-be leader offered opinions only when asked by the group and allowed the leadership of others to come forth.

5. Then ask each manager to share a little about their own experiences of playing out these roles and the reactions and responses they received. Be sure to make the following points and pose the following questions:
  - What were your experiences of performing the task with the different managers?
  - Working together is not always easy. Although experiences with the sharing, or yellow, leader may have led the members of the group to feel like they

17

owned the task, this style of leadership typically causes a group to take longer to accomplish a task because people's opinions and ideas are taken into consideration.
- The sharing style of leadership is useful when there is time available to accomplish the task; when the team is well formed, functioning, and motivated; or when the team has some knowledge and ability to get the job done.
- The sharing style of leadership would be best if you were given the responsibility, for example, to build a park in the town center. You would want to consult the parks and recreation department, a landscaper, some townspeople, especially those with children, and so on, in order to develop a vision and plan for the project, as the park would be something all the townspeople would be able to enjoy.
- The tasks at hand are typically performed at a much faster rate, with the directive, or red, leader because no one is consulted and everyone is directed according to what the leader wants or dictates.
- Sometimes the directed style of leadership is needed, especially in an emergency situation. For example, the last thing anyone would want is for a flight attendant to begin to ask everyone's opinion on how they think she or he should handle the emergency if the airplane was experiencing strong turbulence.
- The directive style of leadership is important when there isn't much time allotted to get a task accomplished or make a decision, when members of the group do not have the knowledge or ability to get the task accomplished, or when the group members do not know one another or have never worked together before.
- The members of a group may be able to pick up the ball and run with it, if they have the skill, or they will become utterly frustrated and give up on the task with the let-it-be leader.
- The let-it-be style of leadership works best when the team is well-functioning and knows one another's strengths and talents, when the team has a good sense of knowledge and the ability to accomplish the task, or when the group knows the process and what to expect.
- The let-it-be style of leadership would be best if you were the leader on a ski trip with a group of ski instructors and the task was to help some young people learn how to ski. In this case, no direction would be needed from you.
- Being a leader does not always mean being the person in charge or the only person with the responsibility. In simpler terms we can say that being a leader does not necessarily mean being the boss.
- Being a leader means knowing when to lead and how to provide direction, consult others, and share responsibilities.
- Being a leader also means knowing when to allow the skills and knowledge of others to provide direction.
- Being a leader means knowing that no one style of leadership can be used in every situation.

6. Provide each of the three groups with a Bible, a sheet of newsprint, and a marker, asking one member of each group to create three columns on the newsprint titling them in this way:

- Column 1: Situation
- Column 2: Style of Leadership
- Column 3: Outcome

You may want to provide them with an example for reference. Then assign each group two of the following Scripture passages:

- Matthew 3:13–17 (the baptism of Jesus)
- Mark 8:27–30 (Peter's declaration about Jesus)
- Luke 5:1–11 (Jesus calls the first disciples)
- John 2:13–16 (Jesus cleanses the Temple)
- John 6:1–15 (feeding the five thousand)
- John 13:1–17 (the washing of the feet)

Invite one person in each group to read each passage out loud. The group's task is to describe (on the newsprint) the situation in each story, identify the style of leadership used, and describe the outcome.

Allow about 15 minutes for the groups to work on this task. Then invite each group to present what they have learned from their Scripture passages.

7. Ask the participants to summarize what they have learned about leadership and what they have learned specifically about Jesus's leadership and the variety of styles he used. Be certain their input includes these key points:

- We see through these Scripture stories that Jesus used different styles of leadership throughout his ministry. Other examples include:
- Jesus used the shared style of leadership when he asked his disciples, "But who do you say that I am?" (Matt. 16:15)
- He used the directive style of leadership when he commissioned the Apostles to continue his mission by saying, "Go therefore and make disciples of all nations, baptizing them in the name of the Father and of the Son and of the Holy Spirit, and teaching them to obey everything that I have commanded you" (Matt. 28:19–20).
- Jesus used the let-it-be style of leadership when he left the decision to the crowd that gathered to stone the woman caught in adultery by allowing the crowd to think and act for itself. Instead of giving the crowd clear direction, he drew on the ground for a while and finally left it with the decision by saying, "Let anyone among you who is without sin be the first to throw a stone at her" (John 8:7).
- We can all follow the example and teachings of Jesus and learn from him.
- Leadership can be offered by anyone, but what makes Christian leaders unique is their focus on and imitation of Christ.

8. Conclude the session by leading the participants in the prayer service, "Prayer of Sending Forth," at the end of this chapter.

Never Too Young to Lead

Ready to Be Empowered: Called to Lead

Overview

Those who are called to lead are often ordinary people who dare to trust God's activity in their lives. They perform simple acts of compassion, forgiveness, acceptance, and love that, in turn, have a tremendously positive effect on the lives of others. We too are called to respond in simple ways by using the gifts God has given us to continue to show the world how to live, just as Jesus did. Saint Teresa of Ávila reminds us that we are Christ's hands and feet in the world.

This session offers opportunities for the young people to participate in one of three options: a visit to a local shrine, an exploration of the life of a Christian leader, or a presentation from a Christian leader in the parish or community.

Preparation

- Gather the following items:
    - ☐ pens and markers, one for each young person
    - ☐ newsprint
- Determine which of the following activities will serve as the "core" of this session. Prepare and plan accordingly. The options include these:
    + Visit a local shrine. Introduce the saint for whom the shrine is named and explain how that person lived as a true Christian leader. Point out the effect his or her style of leadership has had on the world. *Note:* You will need to make prior arrangements with the shrine as well as obtain signed parental permission forms for transportation between the meeting place and the site. You will also need to coordinate transportation.
    + View a video or DVD of anyone whose life and mission has brought light to the world. Some options might include *Great Souls: Mother Teresa* (2002, Vision Video, 56 minutes); *Great Souls: Pope John Paul II* (2002, Vision Video, 56 minutes); *Gift of Hope: The Tony Melendez Story* (2005, Vision Video, 45 minutes); and *The Children's March* (2005, HBO Productions, 40 minute). You will need to obtain a video or DVD for the presentation, a television, and a VCR or a DVD player.
    + Invite a Christian witness within the local community who lives a life of service and love for the good of others. This person may be a director of a homeless shelter or a teen mothers' home or program, or someone who is involved in AIDS ministry, prison ministry, and so on. Outline the specifics you would like the speaker to share, including how Jesus models true leadership for him or her.
- Be prepared to highlight some of the upcoming parish events, activities and programs where the participants can put their leadership skills and qualities to good use. Provide a listing of the various ministries your parish offers, along with contact names and phone numbers, and a brief overview and description of the ministries.
- Prepare a graffiti wall by posting multiple sheets of newsprint on an open wall, covering a large area. Title the wall "Called to Lead."

1. As the young people arrive, distribute a marker to each of them and ask them to approach the graffiti wall. Invite them to decorate it with symbols and writing about what it takes for a person to live as a Christian leader. For example, "It takes courage to be true to who you are" or "reading the Scriptures." They may also include the names of Christian leaders they may know (or may have heard of) whose lives serve as an example in our communities and in our world. You might consider playing some upbeat background music that is appropriate to the theme in order to create a fun, inviting and inspiring environment. Allow about 10 minutes for the participants to create their art.

2. Gather the group and ask them to be seated. Review the graffiti wall the young people created. Ask any appropriate questions to further break open what they've displayed. For example, if "read the Scriptures" is written, ask the group why this would be important or helpful if one is to be a Christian leader in word and action.

3. Continue the session by implementing the option you have preselected (visiting a shrine, showing a DVD, or sharing by a guest speaker). Provide the participants with whatever instructions are needed for the activity of your choosing.

4. Once you have completed your chosen learning activity, invite the young people to ask any questions they may have, either by voicing them aloud—if they feel comfortable doing so—or by writing their questions anonymously on slips of paper that will be collected and shared with the group.

Wrap up the discussion with some specific questions about the Christian leader whose story has been presented, her or his style of leadership, and the effect she or he has had on others. Sample questions might include these:
- How does this person's leadership style imitate that of Jesus?
- How has this person been a creator, a builder, or a restorer?
- What can we put to good use within our own lives from what we have learned about the leadership of this person?

5. Now highlight some of the upcoming parish events, activities, and programs. Provide a listing of the various ministries your parish offers, along with contact names and phone numbers and a brief overview and description of the ministries. Encourage the young people to consider what they might feel called to or what might pique their interest. Circulate a sign-up sheet of interest for the young people to write down their names and contact information and the ministries they may be interested in. Be sure to help connect these young people with the contact person or with another person involved in that area of ministry. This will be highly important, as a mentoring relationship will welcome and nurture the involvement of the young person within the parish community.

6. Conclude the session by leading the participants in the prayer service, "Prayer of Sending Forth," at the end of this chapter.

Never Too Young to Lead

Prayer of Sending Forth

Preparation

- Gather the following items:
  - ☐ THE CATHOLIC YOUTH BIBLE or another Bible
  - ☐ six copies of resource 1, "Intercessions"
  - ☐ table salt, enough for each participant to have a small handful
  - ☐ a small, clear bowl
  - ☐ a large candle and matches
  - ☐ a small cross for the prayer table
  - ☐ a CD of reflective background music and a CD player
- Invite one young person to proclaim Matthew 5:13–16 during the prayer.
- Recruit six volunteers to pray the intercessions. Provide each with a copy of resource 1, "Intercessions," explaining that each volunteer will pray one of the intercessions noted.
- Pour the table salt into the bowl.
- Set the salt, the candle, the Bible, and the small cross on or nearby the prayer table.

1. Invite the group to join you in the prayer space. Play some quiet background music and ask the group to quiet their bodies, minds, and hearts to recognize God's presence within and around them. Begin with the sign of the cross: "In the name of the Father, and of the Son, and of the Holy Spirit. Amen."

2. Inform the participants that your prayer time will focus around the symbols of salt and light. Invite the participants to cup one of their hands to receive a bit of salt, and carefully pour a bit of salt into them. Then offer the following reflection:
- Feel the roughness of the salt in your hands, its grainy texture. Think about the uses for salt and reflect on what salt reminds you of . . . Might it be the sea or your grandmother's cooking?
- Now touch a bit of the salt to your tongue to taste it, and consider the many things salt is used for: to heal wounds, to add flavor to foods, to cure and preserve foods, to exfoliate the skin. Too much of it can cause our blood pressure to rise, and once it has lost its flavor, it is good for nothing. Salt can be used for good . . . or for bad.

3. Invite someone to light the candle. Then continue with these comments:
- Light is used to help us see through the darkness. It is used to give warmth in the cold, but too much of it can blind us from seeing. Light can be used for good or for bad, just like our energy.
- Jesus reminds us that we are the salt of the earth. This means that we add flavor to the world, we can be agents of healing to the wounded, and we can preserve things such as our faith.
- Jesus also tells us that we are the light of the world. In a world where there is darkness, we can bring light. We can bring warmth.

- Called to lead and live as Jesus did, our choices and actions, as well as our attitudes, affect those around us.
- Our leadership, then, is dependent on how we use our energy, and when it is rooted in Christ and used for good, we can lead others to a deeper sense of God and holiness.
- Being called to leadership presumes we have a following, or those that look to us for direction, help and support. Sometimes we may think we are too young to make a difference or an impact on someone else's life, but Jesus and our Church tell us differently. God called young Jeremiah, young Timothy, and Mary, Jesus's own mother, at a young age to share what they had been given and raised them up to be leaders. God can do the same with us.

4. Ask the group to stand, and ask the invited young person to proclaim Matthew 5:13–16. Allow a few moments of silence to follow; then invite the young people to sit and think about the many ways they use their energy and how they are the salt of the earth and the light of the world within their own social circles—with their friends, within their family, at school, on their sports teams, in their clubs, at church, and so on. Ask them to think about how they would like to be salt for the earth and light for the world in the week to come. Allow 2 or 3 minutes for silent reflection.

5. After a brief time, invite the intercessory pray-ers to come forward. Then offer this brief introduction to the prayer:
- As young people gathered in the name of Jesus, we place before the Lord our needs. Together we'll respond, "Lord, hear our prayer."

Present the candle to the first reader and have him or her pray the first intercession noted on resource 1. Then pass the candle to the next pray-er, and so on.

6. Conclude the prayer time by offering the following prayer aloud:
- Lord, we ask you to hear the prayers we've voiced and the personal ones we hold within our hearts. Bless our efforts, and may your Holy Spirit give us the courage to do the right thing and to use our energy for good so that we may truly be the salt of the earth and the light of the world, as you call us to be. Thank you for believing in us, just as we are and for all that we can be, and in our abilities to be creators, builders, and restorers in the world. We ask all this through Christ, our Lord. Amen.

7. End the session with any last-minute announcements. Refreshments may be served at this time.

Intercessions

Reader 1. For the sick in need of the comfort of a friend, we pray that we may be salt for their wounds by offering our time through a visit. Let us pray to the Lord . . .

Reader 2. For those at school whom no one likes, we pray that we may dare to be light by reaching out to them when they are feeling alone. Let us pray to the Lord . . .

Reader 3. For the hungry and the poor in our community, we pray that we may be salt and light for them by helping out at the local soup kitchen, thrift store or homeless shelter. Let us pray to the Lord . . .

Reader 4. For our families, we pray that we may be light by sharing our love with them, even when it seems tough or when we don't want to. Let us pray to the Lord . . .

Reader 5. For ourselves, when we are faced with the temptations that zap our energy and keep us from being salt and light in the world, may your forgiveness and mercy, Lord, wash over us and make us new again. Let us pray to the Lord . . .

Reader 6. In thanksgiving for the gift of Jesus who believes in us and our abilities, we pray that we may come to believe in the goodness in ourselves and our potential to be all that we were created to be and to not be afraid to share it with others, even those we may not know. Let us pray to the Lord . . .

Resource 1: Permission to reproduce is granted. © 2006 by Saint Mary's Press.

2 Listening as a Christian Leader
Ready to Begin: Listening to Others

Overview

Listening is the one activity we do more in life than any other activity except breathing. How much time and energy do we exert in developing the communication skill that has been with us since birth? Christian leaders capitalize on the power of listening. They listen for what people say, what they don't say, and what they would like to say but don't know how to put into words. In this session the young people will be given an opportunity to explore skills to help them become better listeners.

Preparation

- Gather the following items:
  - ☐ newsprint and markers
- Make up a brief story for the game of Telephone, containing many descriptive details to share with the group or groups for the gathering activity in step 1 below. Concoct a different story for each group. You may choose to use any of the following examples:
  + Sarah smiled at Sally, whom she saw at the shoe store on Saturday, and then was bruised when she bumped into Bailey on her way out.
  + The baby birds were nesting on the breaking boughs of the old oak tree while the calico cat, curled up below, licked the morning dew off the new blades of green grass.
  + The cozy campers were startled by the growling grizzly bear who welcomed the morning with a lick of his chops from having devoured the delicious smorgasbord of salami sandwiches and spinach salad.

1. Gather the participants into one large circle. For larger groups, divide into multiple circles of 12 to 15 people. Using these or similar words, briefly introduce the session:
  - We are going to play the old, familiar game of Telephone, during which only a whisper can be used to communicate. I will approach one person in your circle to whom I will tell a brief story.
  - The object of the game is to listen attentively, as this first person will have only one chance to tell the one sitting to her or his right *exactly* what was heard.
  - The sharing continues around the circle. The last person will stand and announce aloud what she or he heard the story to be.

2. When everyone is finished, repeat the game, adding these directions:
  - We're going to try this again, but this time one important aspect will be added.
  - Once the story has been whispered into your ear, you will have just one chance to ask a question of the person who told you the story by whisper-

ing your question to him or her, or to repeat what you heard said in order to have it confirmed. The person who whispered the story to you will be given this one chance to clarify for you with a brief and simple answer. Remember that nothing but a whisper can be used to communicate between the two of you.
- The game will be completed in the same way, with the last person of each circle standing and announcing what he or she heard the story to be.

3. Invite the participants to regather and conduct a large-group discussion using the following questions:
- What was the outcome of the first round of playing Telephone?
- What was the outcome of the second round? What difference did the rule of being able to clarify or ask a question make in the second round?
- What does this game teach us about listening?
- What skills might be important when listening to others?

Conclude the group discussion by asking the participants to quietly think through these questions:
- What characterizes a good listener?
- How can you tell if people are listening to you?

Then offer the following comments:
- Communication is a two-way street, and there are two necessary roles for effective communication: the role of the speaker and the role of the listener.
- Being attentive to the speaker is of the utmost importance, so that we can be sure that we truly hear and understand the speaker's message.
- We can be attentive to others in a variety of ways, from how we use our body language to the words we use to encourage the conversation.
- Because effective communication requires that the listener understand what the speaker is trying to say, reflecting skills are useful. These skills inform the speaker that you understand what she or he is trying to convey, and include summarizing what you heard the speaker say, using her or his exact words or your own by reflecting the speaker's message back to her or him. Reflecting the message back to the speaker is necessary to assure that the message the listener understands is indeed what the speaker is trying to convey.

4. Now ask the participants to think of a time when they were not listened to, and then complete the following sentence with one word:
- When I am not listened to, I feel . . .

Write all the words they come up with on a sheet of newsprint. Then ask them to think of a time when they were listened to, and complete the following sentence in one word:
- When I am listened to, I feel . . .

Write all these words on another sheet of newsprint and compare the two.

5. Continue the large-group discussion by asking the following question:
- In a conversation, how do you show the person who is speaking that you are listening? More specifically, how do you do this without using spoken words? Think of what body language you might use or something you might say to let him or her know you're paying attention.

6. Ask the participants to choose a partner and form pairs. Next, have them demonstrate a true-to-life conversation through role-play, using only nonverbal

examples to show their listening abilities. Ask each pair to take turns with the roles of listener and speaker. Allow a few minutes for each role-play, using these examples:
- a parent informing a teenager of the night's curfew
- a friend telling another friend about a recent breakup
- a student informing a teacher of the reason for her or his tardiness to class

Take a brief moment to ask the participants for more examples of nonverbal communication, so that everyone understands the task. Then allow the role-plays to take place.

7. Now ask the young people to describe the nonverbal "messages" these examples of body language can give. Ask them to identify which skills let the speaker know they are listening, or attending, to him or her. Ask them how these attending skills can be effective, for example, uncrossing one's arms gives the speaker a message of openness and attention from the one who is listening. Continue by asking this next question:
- In a conversation, how do you show the person who is speaking that you "get" what she or he is saying? More specifically, how do you do this with spoken words? What might you say to let the speaker know you understand what is being said?

Now have the pairs role-play the same scenarios, but this time noting that the listener is allowed to use spoken words to respond.

8. Ask the group to describe the verbal messages that were modeled in the role-play. Invite them also to brainstorm other ways of being an attentive listener with spoken words. Then offer these comments:
- We communicate in many other ways than just verbally.
- We communicate through our posture, voice inflection, silence, absence, or lateness, for example.
- Active listening is a skill that as you practice, you will understand more and do better. It is working to understand another person's thoughts and feelings, and verbally reflecting what you understand back to them (almost always in the form of statements) to complete the communication loop.
- It involves reading both verbal and nonverbal communication. It is empathetic in its nature.
- One of the many descriptions of Jesus is "the One who listens." He modeled effective listening as he paid close attention to his disciples, his other followers, and even his antagonists.
- Christians are called to follow in Jesus's footsteps and learn to respond to people as he did. Listening actively is the most basic people-helping skill; the other skills build on and require it.
- When you listen well, you demonstrate to others that their concerns have been heard and understood. As a result, they feel accepted by you, and trust builds.
- Listening is more than just hearing. Effective listening includes hearing, recognizing, interpreting, and comprehending. It's an activity of the ears, eyes, heart, and intellect. The good news is that because listening is a skill, it can be improved by practice. You can learn to be a better listener. Try

incorporating some of these suggestions when you are called to listen to others:

+ *Give your full attention to the other person.* Listen with your ears, eyes, heart, and intellect. Always resist the impulse to turn the conversation to *your* experiences and opinions and to find immediate solutions to problems you may be hearing.
+ *Listen carefully first; problem-solve later.* If the other person has a habit of immediate problem-solving, see if you can help him or her be a better listener and problem explorer.
+ *Keep an open mind.* Try to be honestly interested in what the other person is saying, and be ready to have your own ideas challenged or even changed.
+ *Be willing to consider concepts, ideas and thoughts that are different from yours.* Consciously decide to remove any biases, negative attitudes toward the speaker or the subject, strong differing opinions, self-centeredness, or expectations.
+ *Give the person time to make her or his point before jumping in with your objections.*
+ *Seek clarification.* If you don't know what the other person is talking about, say so at the first opportunity. Listen to the clarification, and if you need further expansion, say so. Make sure you're both focusing on the same thing. Use the reflecting skills to help the speaker clarify.
+ *Try to identify feelings.* If the speaker is expressing feelings, try to understand what he or she is actually feeling. Probe gently, not intrusively, until you do understand. If necessary, tell the speaker that you're trying to better understand what he or she is feeling.
+ *Listen to one person at a time.* If you're in a group and more than one person is talking at a time, select one to listen to fully rather than giving part of your attention to each speaker.
+ *Listen to nature.* Work at improving your listening skills by seeking quiet times when you can really listen to nature. See how much more keenly you'll discriminate among noises in your environment, and how you'll learn to appreciate silence.
+ *Listen to yourself.* Become aware of your feelings and thoughts when you're doing your favorite things, when you're about to try something new, and so on. Pay attention to these thoughts and feelings, and further explore them on your own. Create time in your day to acknowledge, express, and explore your thoughts and feelings.
+ *Listen to God.* Create space in your life to listen to God. Study the Scriptures, seek God's guidance in prayer and meditation, and listen to the advice of trusted friends.

9. Conclude by inviting the participants to offer any additional suggestions they might have for better listening. Challenge them to practice these skills with friends and family members in an effort to improve their listening abilities. End the session by leading the participants in the prayer service, "Prayer of Sending Forth," at the end of this chapter.

Ready to Be Formed: Listening to God

Overview

We live in a world of noise. Almost everywhere we go, we find sounds competing with our minds, keeping us from letting our thoughts get below the surface level. Hearing God's voice means not listening to the noise of the world around us. Within this session the young people will be given an experience of three different forms of personal prayer to help them discover a method that leads them to the art of listening to God.

Preparation

- Gather the following items:
    - ☐ newsprint and markers
    - ☐ masking tape
    - ☐ various appropriate magazines from which to take clippings, at least one for each participant
    - ☐ scissors and glue sticks, enough for all the participants
    - ☐ a stopwatch or timer
- Prepare a graffiti wall by posting a large section of newsprint on a wall. On one section of the wall, draw a large set of lips, and on another section, draw a large ear. Be sure to leave lots of room for clippings, drawings, and words to fit within its drawn outline. At the top of the mouth, print the words, "What is prayer when I'm the speaker?" At the top of the ear, print, "What is prayer when I'm the listener?" You may want to add a couple of examples to aid them, such as (under "prayer for the speaker") "It's about letting God know all of what's on your mind," or (under "prayer for the listener") "It's sometimes frustrating because God isn't responding right away." Place the markers, magazines, scissors, and glue sticks nearby.
- Recruit two adults or team members to facilitate one of the prayer experiences. Review with the volunteers the experience as outlined in resource 2, "Prayer Stations."

   1. As the young people arrive, invite them to approach the graffiti wall. Direct them to decorate both the mouth and the ear with symbols, magazine clippings, and writing that pertains to the questions on the newsprint. Allow a few minutes for them to create their "art."

   2. Gather the participants and invite them to be seated and get settled in. Then review and summarize the points about prayer made on the graffiti wall they've created. Ask any appropriate questions to further break open what they've displayed. For example, if they've mentioned that listening in prayer can be frustrating, ask them why and how they know that God has heard their prayer, or if they say that prayer for the speaker is great because God never cuts them off in conversation, ask why that is important to them and how not cutting off someone in a conversation might make the speaker feel? To summarize the discussion, make the following points in these or your own words:

- Prayer is a conversation between you and God. Within this conversation is a speaker and a listener, both roles performed by both the people involved in the dialogue.
- You might wonder what listening to and communicating with God has to do with becoming an even better listener and communicator.
- Jesus, who was the ultimate leader, kept in constant contact with his Father; in fact, he did so daily. It is equally as important for us, as leaders, to "be in touch" with God on a daily basis—not just to talk with God but to take the time to listen.
- Only through our connection with God can we come to know ourselves better, as God knows us, and how to best use the talents, skills, and abilities God has given each of us.
- Only God knows what you at your ultimate best looks like. That is why we need to connect with and listen attentively to God.
- We see in the Scriptures that even Jesus took time away from the crowds and his closest friends and family to be alone with God and to listen to God so that he could return to his ministry renewed and refocused.
- It was through listening to God and growing in faith that Jesus came to realize his mission and found the strength to live it.
- True Christian leaders take the time (and make the time) to communicate and "stay in touch" with God, who guides and directs them. Because Jesus kept in touch with his Father, so too must we.

3. Separate the participants into two groups. Then offer the following directions:
- You are about to take part in two experiences that will offer you the opportunity to be in touch with God. Each group will be given 15 minutes for each experience.
- I encourage you to open your hearts and minds to the experiences so that you may be able to listen to God with your entire being.
- When the buzzer rings, please move on to the second station.
- Remember that the goal is direct communication—to speak with God—but also to take the time to really listen and be attentive to God and the message God has for you, whether that is a word, an idea, an image, or a feeling.

4. To begin, offer the following prayer:
- Come, Holy Spirit, open our minds, ears, and hearts to hear your word for us and within us. Quiet our minds and hearts so that we may be attentive to you. We thank you for hearing our prayer, always, and for your patience with us in times when we are distracted from hearing your voice. Come, Holy Spirit, and prepare us to hear your word. Amen.

5. Direct each group to the first prayer station. Once everyone is settled, set the timer for 15 minutes. When 15 minutes has passed, direct the groups to their next prayer experience. When the two experiences are completed, direct the groups to regather in the large group. Invite volunteers to share one of their prayer experiences with the large group. You can do so by posing simple questions like these:
- Which experience was your favorite? Why?
- Which was more challenging for you? Why?
- Which experience allowed you to listen better to God? Why?

Listening as a Christian Leader

- Why do you think prayer is an important element in the life of a Christian leader?

6. After a few minutes of sharing, offer the following comments:
- When present, God speaks in many different ways. God may leave you with a feeling, an idea, a thought, a word, or simply silence. God's time with you may be more about just being in each other's company, like two friends who do not need to talk all the time but who share moments of just being together.
- Jesus reminds us, "apart from me you can do nothing" (John 15:5).
- Only through daily connection to God can we come to know God's will for us—to where and what we are called.
- Through prayer Jesus came to realize just who he was, as well as his purpose and mission here on earth. None of us is born with that knowledge, not even Jesus. Instead, we must grow into the truth of who we are by seeking it.
- What we need to remember is that we cannot live out our purpose unless we seek to connect with our Creator, for it is God who truly knows our best selves and the difference we can make in this world.
- Prayer was a priority for Jesus. He never left it to chance or to how he was feeling. He was faithful to it. It must be so for us as well. Listening to God through prayer, then, is step one in Christian leadership.

7. Wrap up the session by leading the participants in a brainstorming session on ideas they can use in their daily lives to be more attentive to God's voice by asking the following question:
- How can we discipline ourselves to hear the voice of God?

Some ideas might include these:
- Plan ahead. Restructure your schedule so you can spend uninterrupted time with God. Find a quiet place and bring along your Bible, notebook, and pen.
- Prepare yourself mentally, emotionally, and physically. It is essential that we come to God with an open heart and a desire to truly listen.
- Spend time in prayer, liturgy, Scripture reading, and meditation on God's word. As you read God's word, ask God to speak to you.
- Wait expectantly. This is not a time to zone out or think of the activities for later in the day. If something apart from God's voice comes to your mind, jot it down. This will free your mind to be able to concentrate on God. Spend time in silence, waiting for God to speak in your spirit. Feel free to ask God questions, and then await an answer.
- Some people like to write down what they hear from God or any direction they receive about a certain issue.
- Continue your time of waiting on God throughout the day. Always be listening for God's voice

8. Conclude the brainstorming activity and the session by noting the following:
- Listening to God is an important part of the Christian leader's life. God desires to speak to us, and we have the privilege of listening to God's instruction and guidance.
- Prayer is not a way of making use of God; prayer is a way of offering ourselves to God so that God is able to make use of us.
- It may be that one of our great faults in prayer is that we talk too much and listen too little.

Ready to Be Empowered: A Way of Listening

Overview

The purpose of this session is to provide the young people with an example of how a Christian leader lives the commitment of effective communication with others and with God in daily life through reflecting on and breaking open the Scriptures both as individuals and with others.

Preparation

- Gather the following items:
  - ☐ copies of handout 1, "My Two Cents," one for each participant
  - ☐ pens or pencils, one for each participant
  - ☐ THE CATHOLIC YOUTH BIBLE or another Bible, one for each small group of six to eight people
  - ☐ paper for journaling

1. As the young people arrive, distribute handout 1, "My Two Cents," to each participant, along with a pen or pencil. Encourage them to mill around, acquiring answers to the questions on their handouts from as many different people as possible. Allow 10 minutes for the activity.

2. Gather the participants for a large-group sharing of what they've learned about others in the group. Go through each of the questions on the handout, asking the participants to share the answers written by others, though to respect everyone's anonymity, no names should be revealed.

3. Offer the following points in these or your own words:
- Just as our gathering activity gave us the opportunity to get to know more about other people in the group, prayer allows us to share with God our thoughts and feelings, as well as to hear God's word for us and our lives.
- We know that Jesus often turned to the Holy Scriptures for guidance in his earthly life. We also know that Jesus often took time to pray and to reference Old Testament teachings and law.
- Praying and sharing the Scriptures are central characteristics of the Christian leader. Like Jesus, we too can look to the Scriptures to provide us with guidance, direction, accountability, hope, and vision.
- The remainder of the session will be devoted to learning a method of prayer using the sacred Scriptures.
- The method of prayer we will experience is called *lectio divina,* which means "holy reading," and was given to us by Saint Benedict.
- *Lectio divina* is a method of praying with the Scriptures, and has five parts to it:
  + First, we will read the passage and allow ourselves to receive it and be open to it.
  + Second, we will allow ourselves to think about the word of God we've just heard, engaging our mind and heart.
  + Third, we will respond to God through prayer by beginning a conversation with him in our heart or through writing or drawing.

- + Fourth, we will allow ourselves to sit with God's word quietly and to rest in it, to be absorbed by it, and to feel God's love through it. In this step no words are necessary. It is just about "being" in the moment.
- + Last, we will respond to God's word for us through action, by the way we will live our life now that we've received this important word from God. Just as lives has no effect until it is shared and acted on, it is the same with God's word; we give life to it.
- + As young Christians called to be leaders within the Church and in our world, listening to and acting on God's word is our mission in life, through virtue of our baptism as members of the Body of Christ.

4. Divide the participants into small groups of six to eight people. Provide each group with a Bible and ask one member of each group to find Luke 5:1–11. Once the groups are settled, begin the process by offering the following prayer:

- ○ Come, Holy Spirit, open our minds, ears, and hearts to hear your word for us and within us. Quiet our minds and hearts so that we may be attentive to you. We thank you for hearing our prayer, always, and for your patience with us in times when we are distracted from hearing your voice. Come, Holy Spirit, and prepare us to hear your word. Amen.

5. Facilitate the process by following the steps outlined below:
- Invite someone in each group to read the passage from the Scriptures. Allow for a brief moment of silence. Now ask the participants to be attentive to a word or phrase that may jump out at them as a different person rereads the passage.
- Invite the participants to reflect on the passage, including the word or phrase that stood out to them.
- Ask: How does this word or phrase relate to your life right now? What might be God's message for you through this word, phrase, and passage? How does this make you feel?
- Invite the participants to engage in a conversation with God for a moment, to share with him their feelings and thoughts about his word for them. Ask them to be attentive to how God may respond in the conversation. They may choose to sit quietly or to write out their conversation. Last, ask them to offer to God the parts of them that were touched by his word so that these same parts will help them to be transformed by God's word.
- After a few moments, ask the participants to rest quietly in God's presence, where no words are needed. Invite them to be loved by God in this moment and to bask in God's message for them, or in the feeling they are experiencing.
- Conclude by asking the participants to consider how God's word may be calling them to action, and have them write this down.

6. Facilitate informal small-group sharing, inviting the participants to share their experiences. Recall the different parts of the prayer and ask some questions appropriate to each step in the process for sharing. Some opening questions for sharing might include these:
- How would you describe what you just experienced and why?
- What did you like about this experience of praying with God's word?
- How might this process, *lectio divina*, help you connect with God and others on a more intimate level of faith?
- How does praying with the Scriptures help the Christian leader be more effective?

7. Evaluate the overall experience of this prayer and how the young people believe *lectio divina* can become a helpful method of prayer for them and also in their lives as Christian leaders. Conclude by reviewing some of the other types of prayer the young people enjoy and practice, as well as some others that are also available to them.

Prayer of Sending Forth

Preparation

- Gather the following items:
  - ☐ reflective instrumental background music
  - ☐ a CD player
- Create a quiet space for the prayer, dimming the lighting and assuring plenty of floor space for the participants to lie down without being in too-close proximity of another person.

1. Play some reflective music softly. Before you invite the participants to join you in a space for prayer, explain the following to them:
- The prayer we are about to experience is called guided meditation. The experience begins by relaxing and quieting the body, mind, and soul to prepare to be as present to God as we can, open to hearing his word. This will require your participation, but through absolute silence.

2. Now invite them into the prayer space, asking all of them to find their own space on the floor and to lie on their backs. Ask them to remain still, quieting their bodies, minds, and hearts to recognize God's presence within and around them.

3. When everyone has settled, explain the following:
- You are about to have an experience of personal prayer. Personal prayer is that which happens between you and God. It requires no one else's participation. Although everyone is gathered here to experience the guided meditation, each person will experience this prayer individually. It will be a personal connection between you and God.

4. Begin the guided meditation as noted below. Be sure to speak slowly and pause as indicated by the ellipses.
- Let's begin by getting comfortable in your own space. . . . Take a slow breath or two, and gently close your eyes. . . . Now take a deep breath, when you are ready, and hold it for a moment; then let it all out and begin to feel the tension of the day leave you as you exhale. Let go of anything within you that has kept you from a sense of peace and ease. . . .
- Tense up the muscles in your body and hold them tight for a moment, now release them and feel your body relax even more.
- Take another breath, a deep breath, letting even more tension go and leave your body, your mind, and your spirit . . . and feel your whole self become more and more relaxed.
- Remind yourself that is it okay to relax here, in this place and at this time. . . . There is no other place you have to be right now, nothing else you have to do right now. . . . You can relax, fully and completely.
- Take a last deep breath, hold it, then let it go, and allow your body to resume its normal, yet relaxed, rhythm of breathing.
- Now imagine yourself walking along a path. This can be any path—one in the woods, on the beach, or through a garden. Feel the brush, dust, sand, or pebbles kick up behind you as you stroll along. Notice your surroundings—the shrubbery or flowers at your feet, the water rolling in by the

- waves. Hear the sounds of the birds and other creatures that share your path. Be at peace and enjoy your stroll, taking in the beauty of nature that surrounds you.
  - As you walk along, you begin to hear the gentle footsteps of someone approaching from behind. You do not feel anxious about this, because this person's presence brings a comforting and peaceful sense. As you turn to notice, you recognize this person as Jesus. Happy to see you, the two of you embrace like old friends. Feel the embrace of Jesus. . . . Walk along this path together, and share with Jesus all that is happening in your life right now—your excitements and joys, your fears, your disappointments. Take the time now to just walk and be with Jesus. . . .
  - As the path seems to come to an end, you notice that Jesus has led you to an open meadow—and a beautiful and lush one it is—full of color and tall grass, and the flowers are abundant, so much so that you can smell their fragrance. Listen now to what Jesus has to say to you. . . .
  - Jesus isn't quite finished with what he has in store for you. As he shows you the open meadow, you notice a rock in the near distance with words written on it, which read, "Your treasure lies beneath." Curious, you begin to dig. The soil is soft and easy to brush away. As you continue to dig, you finally come to what seems to be a treasure box. Brush more of the soil away, as if to loosen it from the ground. Pull the box out of the ground. Carefully open it, and let your eyes search for the gift inside. What do you see? . . . What is the gift Jesus has for you in your life right now? . . .
  - Hear Jesus tell you how much you are loved, how much he depends on you to be his eyes, ears, hands, and feet in the world. Hear him tell you how much he truly believes in you. This gift is for you to take, so carefully remove it from the box. Jesus asks you to return the treasure box to the ground for another day, when there will be more gifts for you to uncover. Return the box to the ground and gently cover it with the soil.
  - As you motion to get up, Jesus leads you back to the path, yet in the meantime, you notice that Jesus has left your side, but his presence has not. Continue back on your path, reflecting on this gift from Jesus. How does this gift make you feel? How can you use this gift in your life right now?
  - Let your path slowly lead you back to this room. When you're ready, slowly open your eyes and carefully sit up, remaining silent and reflective. There is no rush. We will wait for you.
  - Now turn to one partner and share what you found in your treasure box. If you prefer not to share, you are welcome to come forward and get a blank sheet of paper and a pen and do some journaling.
  - How does this gift make you feel, and what will you do with this gift from Jesus?

5. After some sharing, say the following:
  - The Lord is with you (and also with you). Let us end our time of prayer together, "In the name of the Father . . ." and with a sign of Christ's peace (make the sign of the cross).

6. End the session with any last-minute announcements. Refreshments may be served at this time.

Prayer Stations

Praying with Music

Before the session select a contemporary, top-forty song that is familiar to the young people and delivers a positive message through its lyrics. Reflect on its message and connect it to the message of the Gospel. Provide the participants with a copy of the lyrics for reflection.

Introduce the experience by making the following point:
- God speaks to us in a variety of ways, and sometimes it is through the ordinary, whether that is the voice of a friend, a phrase in a book we're reading, or through a song on the radio. When these engage our hearts and challenge us to goodness, it's a pretty good guess that God is speaking.

Next, briefly introduce the song and its message, making a brief connection to the message of the Gospel. Ask the participants to be attentive to the experience and to God's voice through the song. Now play the song.

Allow for a few moments of silence and invite the participants to reflect on what they heard in the song and how they would like to respond to God in prayer.

Conclude by inviting the participants to open to a blank journal page and to write or draw about their prayer experience and what they heard, as well as how they might respond to what they heard.

Praying Through Meditation

The purpose of this experience of prayer is to provide a variety of options to the participants from which to choose to experience this type of prayer for themselves. Before the session you will need to provide a written copy of one of the mysteries of the rosary; a written quotation from the Scriptures, like: "My sheep hear my voice. I know them, and they follow me" (John 10:27); and a few objects from nature, like a large rock or a branch; along with some questions to help them reflect, like: "What does this object of nature symbolize? What is its purpose? How does it reflect God to you? How are you like the object? If the object had a voice, what would it tell you about life and how to live it? What would it tell you of God?"

Introduce the segment by making the following points:
- Praying through meditation is about quieting and focusing our minds, hearts, and bodies on an object, a word, a rhythm, or an image that helps us meet God within at a deeper and more intimate level, where we both listen to and talk with God.
- Provided for you are a variety of methods to lead you to a deeper experience of God and hearing God's voice: a mystery of the rosary, a quotation from the Scriptures or an object from nature. Choose one, go off into a space of your own, and enter into the prayer. Be sure to allow yourself the time and space to quiet yourself and to focus on the prayer, which will help you to focus on God and lead you to a deeper intimacy with him. Conclude by writing or drawing about your experience—what you heard and how you will respond to God's message for you.

Resource 2: Permission to reproduce is granted. © 2006 by Saint Mary's Press.

My Two Cents

A song that I really connect with right now is _____ because _____.

Someone in my life who is a good listener is _____ (their name and relationship to you).

_____ is one of my best teachers.

_____ loves me for who I am, no matter what.

Someone I'd like to be more like is _____ (their name and relationship to you), because _____.

Something that makes me nervous is _____.

What I fear most is _____ because _____.

Lately I've been thinking a lot about _____.

I wish I could better understand _____ because _____.

My favorite story from the Scriptures is _____ because _____.

My favorite charity is _____ because _____.

I think young people today _____.

My hero is _____.

When I grow up, I'd like to be _____.

One thing I am most grateful for is _____ because _____.

One thing I'd like to change if I could is _____.

People who know me well would say that one of my best attributes is _____.

One thing I think I do well is _____.

One person I truly trust and believe in is _____ (their name and relationship to you).

One thing I truly believe is _____ because _____.

Handout 1: Permission to reproduce is granted. © 2006 by Saint Mary's Press.

3 Conflict Resolution
Ready to Begin: How We Approach Conflict

Overview

Whether conflict is called fighting, arguing, disagreeing, enjoying a difference of opinion, engaging in a confrontation, feuding, or battling, it is an inevitable part of human relationships. In this session the participants explore healthy methods of conflict resolution in which both parties win.

Preparation

- Gather the following items:
  - ☐ buttons (or beans), enough for each participant to have several of them
  - ☐ pens or pencils
  - ☐ copies of handout 2, "My Style," one for each participant

1. Divide the participants into groups of five. Distribute a few buttons to each person. Be sure to give some participants more buttons and some fewer. Explain that the purpose of the game is simply, "Whichever team has the most buttons at the end of 2 minutes wins. Participants may trade, bargain, and otherwise negotiate to get buttons from other players." You'll want to note that this activity is not meant to get physical. The only way to obtain the buttons is through negotiation and discussion, not physical contact. Once everyone understands the rules, begin the game. After 2 minutes, stop the play. Have the participants count their buttons and announce the winner.

2. Lead the participants in a brief discussion using some of the following questions:
- How did you feel playing this game? Why?
- How was it like a real conflict situation?
- Was there a problem with the instructions? (Not enough information?)
- Does that happen in real life?
- Did you feel like someone wasn't playing fair? Were there any rules?
- What unspoken rules did everyone accept? (Not physically hurting others? Staying within your group?)
- Did anything happen to make you angry?
- What did you do when you got angry?
- What different methods were used to get the buttons?
- Who tried intimidation? negotiation? ganging up?

3. Summarize the game with the following key points:
- Just as competition occurs in everybody's life, so does conflict. People simply disagree, and often when they try to settle their differences, someone wins and someone loses.

○ Nobody likes to lose, but at one time or another in life, everyone loses. Nobody likes conflict either, but conflicts do happen.

4. Regather in the large group and provide each participant with a pen or pencil and a copy of handout 2, "My Style." Read the directions at the beginning of the activity and emphasize the importance of marking their first reaction. If the participants ask about circling more than one letter for each situation, tell them to circle only the one that indicates what they would do if they did not consider consequences; this will yield their most natural response. Point out that this activity calls them to respond before they think. Give the young people about 10 minutes to complete the handout.

5. When all the participants have finished marking their responses, direct them to the scoring grid on the handout and have them read the directions there. Use your own responses as an example to show them how to discover their style. Give everyone 2 to 3 minutes to score their responses and identify their style of handling conflict.

6. Introduce the material on styles of conflict management as noted below, emphasizing that these explanations can help the participants understand and identify various conflict-management styles.

- *Avoid.* (It's no problem.) Some people do not like to argue or fight. They even physically move away from disagreements. Or if a disagreement is right in front of their nose, they act as if it does not exist.
    + Sometimes people must avoid conflicts—for example, when they judge that the time is not right or that they need someone else to help solve the problem, or that the problem just is not worth fighting about.
    + However, avoiding disagreements at any cost means always losing. Avoiders never even try to get what they really want. When avoiders always lose, someone else always wins.
- *Work against.* (Wanna fight about it?) Some people always choose fighting as their first option. They physically move toward disagreements and focus on winning at the expense of another.
    + Sometimes competition is the appropriate way to settle a disagreement. For example, a sports competition is the best way to settle a disagreement about which team is better.
    + A fight or an argument is a competition in which one person or group tries to overpower another. When this kind of conflict resolution occurs, someone always wins and someone always loses.
- *Work together.* (Let's each contribute something.) Working together is probably the best way to handle most conflicts because both sides win. Everybody is satisfied with the solution because everyone has given something and everyone has received something.
- *Meet halfway* (You win some; you lose some.) Meeting halfway can be good sometimes because both sides end up winning something, but they end up losing something too. This is a fair way of dealing with choices that people have to make together. It works best when everybody realizes that both sides will lose something.

These four ways of dealing with disagreements are all useful and even necessary some of the time. In facing a conflict, first decide if the situation calls for a clear

winner or loser. Most conflicts do not call for a winner and a loser; most call for winners. When that is the case, work to resolve the conflict so that everybody wins—because nobody likes to lose.
- Remember these things:
  + Conflict is inevitable. How you handle conflict is your choice.
  + The easy way out is not always the best way. It may be easy to walk away from a conflict or to be aggressive and fight, but in either case someone will end up losing and getting hurt.
  + Apologize to people you hurt. Forgive those who hurt you.
  + Be kind—every single moment of your life.

7. Separate the participants into small groups, asking each group to develop a skit that will display a real-life scenario of conflict. Some examples might include a conflict between siblings, a conflict between two friends, a conflict between parent and child, a conflict about money, a conflict within a group of people, and so on. Assign each group one or two styles of resolution. Tell the groups to work together to come up with a separate conclusion to the scenario that reflects each style of conflict management they were assigned. They will need to choose one of the styles of resolution you previously presented. Encourage the participants' creativity and use of props.

8. After 10 to 15 minutes has passed, call the group back together and ask each group to come forward and share their role-play with the larger group. Invite conversation after each skit to discuss alternate approaches to the conflict. Bring this activity to a close by noting that most often both sides in a conflict can end up winning in some way. Note also that if one of the parties in a conflict refuses to cooperate, nothing can be done. Ask the participants how they would handle a situation in which one party refuses to negotiate. Look for answers such as allowing for a cooling-off period or looking for a better time and place to solve the problem.

9. Then offer some final thoughts along these lines:
  ○ No one likes conflict, though it is an occurrence in everyone's life. The Christian leader is committed to seeking resolution by inviting those involved to do the same, even when resolution may not occur. Look to how Jesus approached conflict—use gentleness, compassion, and mercy, and stand in the truth—never forcefully, but through invitation and challenge.
  ○ For the Christian leader, the commitment to seek resolution to conflict, rather than avoid it, is rooted in the mission of Jesus. Jesus sought to understand people and their situations by listening, speaking the truth, forgiving, and challenging them to see a better way. We are called to do the same.

10. Conclude the session by leading the participants in the prayer service, "Prayer of Sending Forth," at the end of this chapter.

(Portions of this session are adapted from Kielbasa, *Dealing with Tough Times*, p. 52, and *Dealing with Tough Times* student workbook, pp. 16–19.)

Ready to Be Formed: Mediation

Overview

This session takes the young people beyond themselves and their personal relationships, into the communities and organizations where they lead. The session will enable them to develop the skills they need to help mediate disputes between individuals or groups.

Preparation

- Gather the following items:
  - ☐ newsprint and markers
  - ☐ one copy of resource 3, "Conflict Case Studies"
  - ☐ copies of handout 3, "The Mediation Process," one for each participant
  - ☐ blank paper, one sheet for each participant
  - ☐ pens or pencils
- Outline the mediation process on newsprint as follows:
  + Step 1: Telling the story—just the facts
  + Step 2: Telling the story—how the parties feel
  + Step 3: Brainstorming for solutions
  + Step 4: Choosing the best solution
  + Step 5: Looking to the future
- Cut apart resource 3 as directed on the resource.

1. Divide the participants into an even number of small groups, with two to four people in each group. Give each group a piece of newsprint and a variety of markers. Explain that each group will be an automotive design team, and its task will be to design one half of a car. Designate half the groups to design the front half of a car and the remaining groups to design the rear half of a car. Tell the participants that they will have about 10 minutes to complete their design and that it is against the rules to look at another group's design.

Instruct the groups to begin. Alert them when they have only 1 minute left to complete their work.

2. When time is up, combine each group that has a design for the front of a car with a group that has a design for the rear of a car. Tell each new group to prepare a sales presentation identifying the best features of its combined design. The group will then try to convince the other participants that its creation is the best total car and that they should buy it.

Allow the groups about 5 minutes to prepare their sales presentations.

3. Gather the groups together and ask them to take turns giving their sales presentations. After all the groups have presented their sales talks, ask all the participants to vote for the car design they would most like to purchase.

4. When the voting is completed, use the following questions to lead a discussion of the activity:
  - ○ What would have made the process of designing a complete car, front and back, more successful? [The group may suggest things like seeing what the

other group was doing, cooperating on the design, and being able to talk together.]
- Did everyone vote for their own design? If so, why? [The young people may talk about wanting to win and may mention that people always want to convince others that their own ideas are best.]
- When the groups designing the front and rear halves of a car combined, was there a sense of competition about which qualities would be stressed in the sales presentation?

5. Point out that when groups of people are in conflict, too often they automatically fall into a competitive attitude toward one another. It is taken for granted that one party must win and others lose. True resolution occurs when the people in a dispute come together to find solutions that produce a win-win situation.

Then ask the young people to brainstorm some answers to the following questions:
- What are the obstacles to achieving win-win situations?
- Why are we competitive?

Conclude by noting that peace does not equal the absence of conflict; peace does equal win-win solutions to conflict.

(This exercise is based on the activity "Car Auction," in Bianchi, Butler, and Richey, *Warm-ups for Meeting Leaders,* p. 107.)

6. Remind the young people that conflict and the feelings conflict raises are a normal part of life, and that helping others deal with conflict in a positive way is something we can do as Christian leaders.

7. Ask the participants to quickly identify the different groups to which they belong. These should include family, school, and community groups. List the young people's responses on a piece of newsprint. Explain that conflict occurs not only between individuals in groups but also between groups.

8. Explain the following points in your own words:
- Many times individuals or groups involved in conflict are unable to solve the situation by themselves because of feelings of anger, frustration, or competitiveness. When this is the case, the parties in conflict may turn to a process called mediation, where another person or group acts as an impartial umpire and tries to settle the dispute.
- The goal of mediation is resolving the conflict, not placing blame or winning the argument.
- For mediation to be successful, all parties must want to settle the conflict and must agree to tell the truth and listen and show respect for others.

9. Call the group's attention to the newsprint listing the five-step process for mediating a conflict. Using the following material, explain each step:
- Step 1: Telling the story—just the facts
  + Ask each party to tell honestly what happened. This identifies the problem. A conflict cannot be resolved unless the parties involved agree about what the problem really is.
  + Listen to each party tell his or her version of what happened without interruption. The cause of conflict may be that those involved have different ver-

sions of what really happened.
- Step 2: Telling the story—how the parties feel
  + Ask the parties to share how they feel about what happened, and why. Emotions play an important part in conflict, and everyone's feelings must be treated with respect.
  + Ask each party if she or he understands why the other parties feel as they do.
- Step 3: Brainstorming for solutions
  + Remind the parties that mediation is about finding a win-win solution that is fair to all parties; it is not about some particular party's winning or losing.
  + Ask all the parties to think of as many ways as possible to solve this conflict. Write down their responses.
- Step 4: Choosing the best solution
  + Ask the parties which possible solutions they like best.
  + Ask the parties which solutions they feel they can agree to.
  + Make sure the solutions the parties agree to are realistic and doable.
  + If all the parties can agree to one of the suggested solutions, declare the dispute settled. If all the parties cannot agree to one of the suggested solutions, declare that the dispute cannot be settled. The parties in an unresolved dispute now may look for another solution, or they may opt out of the mediation process and continue the conflict. Choosing the latter course may indicate that angry feelings have not been put to rest or that the parties do not really want to resolve the conflict at this time.
- Step 5: Looking to the future
  + Ask the parties for ideas on how to prevent this conflict from happening again.

(This process is adapted from Schmidt, *Mediation* teacher's guide, pp. 28–29.)

10. Ask the participants if they have any questions or comments about the process of mediation. Tell them that next they will be putting this process to use by acting as mediators to resolve conflicts in case studies based on actual situations involving young people their age.

11. Divide the participants into four small groups. Give each group a copy of a situation from resource 3, "Conflict Case Studies." Give each participant a copy of handout 3, "The Mediation Process." Also distribute a blank sheet of paper and a pen or pencil to each participant.

12. Instruct the groups to read and discuss their situations. Ask them to pretend they are a team of mediators, and have them prepare a report showing how each step of the mediation process could be used to solve the conflict in their case study. Give them 10 minutes to work on their presentations.

13. When all the groups have finished preparing their reports, invite them to take turns explaining their case study to the other participants and describing how they would mediate it. After each presentation ask the whole group for additional ideas about how this conflict might be avoided in the future.

14. After all the presentations have been made and discussed, ask the participants how they feel about using the mediation process and how it relates to leadership. Then challenge the participants to look for places and situations where they can put these skills to use—in their families, schools, teams, and other groups.

15. Conclude the session by conducting the prayer service, "Prayer of Sending Forth," at the end of the chapter.

Ready to Be Empowered: Forgiveness and Conflict

Overview

Conflict resolution for the Christian is really about respecting others, as well as offering and seeking forgiveness and reconciliation when possible. The responsibility of the Christian leader is to seek to be an instrument of forgiveness, reconciliation, and resolution. This session will invite the young people to consider this awesome yet challenging responsibility through the use of the Scriptures, through role-playing, and in reflecting on a situation in their lives where there is a need for forgiveness.

Preparation

- Gather the following items:
    - ☐ newsprint and markers
    - ☐ masking tape
    - ☐ THE CATHOLIC YOUTH BIBLE or another Bible
    - ☐ pens or pencils
    - ☐ notecard-sized pieces of paper, one for each participant
    - ☐ a small basket
- Designate locations throughout the room for teams of no more than six to situate themselves. In those locations place four sheets of newsprint and one marker for each participant.
- Write the following scenarios on a sheet or two of newsprint:
    + a student confronting a teacher for a better grade on a paper, which he or she feels is well deserved
    + a parent confronting a child because his or her room is not, yet, cleaned
    + a teenager confronting a clerk regarding having been shortchanged
    + a coach confronting a team member for being late for practice

1. As the participants arrive, assign them to one of the small-group areas that you set up before the session. When everyone has been assigned to a group, tell the participants that they are going to engage in a friendly competition. Explain that you will name a category, and then the groups will have 1 minute to brainstorm and write on their sheets of newsprint as many answers as they can that fit the category. They will score one point for each answer not duplicated by another group.

2. When you are certain they understand the directions, read the first category in the following list. Allow a minute for brainstorming and writing. After the minute is up, have the groups post their newsprint and compare their answers. Cross out any duplicate items on the newsprint sheets and count the items that remain. Score one point for every answer that is not crossed out. Proceed in this manner for each of the next four categories:
- things friends argue about
- things people say during an argument
- things that need two people to work well
- things parents say to break up an argument between siblings

3. When you have finished the brainstorming, tally the results and announce the winning group. Then ask the participants if anyone can suggest the theme that ran through the categories. Explain that in every relationship, no matter how strong, people sometimes have to deal with disagreements and differences. Continue by offering the following key points:

- Whenever there is conflict, feelings often get hurt and words are said or actions are taken that cause harm to the relationship. One important practice of a Christian leader is to take responsibility when she or he has done something wrong or when she or he has hurt someone, whether physically (fist fighting), emotionally (putting someone down), or spiritually (leading someone to sin).
- A Christian leader takes responsibility for seeking and offering forgiveness, especially when it is most difficult. (You may choose to share a personal story or that of Pope John Paul II, who sought reconciliation with the man who shot him, as well as forgiveness for the anger he harbored against the man!)
- Being in conflict with another person does not necessarily mean that sin is involved and that forgiveness needs to be offered or received. It is okay to disagree with someone and to have a differing opinion or belief. There are times when people hold different perspectives and don't see eye-to-eye. That is not sinful, though one important aspect when dealing with conflict like this is to offer respect to someone whose ideas, thoughts, or decisions may be different from your own. Even when we do not agree, we are called to respect others; respect, in this case, is the resolution and common ground on which we can all stand, no matter what our differences may be.
- Respecting others with differing opinions and ideas is not about striving to get them to see another way or your way. Mutual respect is about allowing both sides to be heard, offering attention, and not demanding that either side "join one camp." Even though you may not accept or believe in another person's ideas, opinions, or beliefs, respect is shown by holding back any ridicule or argument. Mutual respect is shown when the opinions and beliefs of all are allowed to be shared and voiced.
- Respecting others does not mean that one has to abandon her or his own opinions, ideas, or beliefs that may differ with those of other people. Respect shows consideration for another, recognizing that all people are creations of God, where all are equal but not necessarily the same.
- How many of you have had an argument with your parents? Have any of you ever had a falling out with a friend? During our time together, we are going to look at a way to work toward resolution when conflict arises.
- There is a formula for resolving conflict. It involves using what are called "I statements."
- Instead of confronting the person you're in conflict with by blaming him or her or making lots of "you, you, you" statements, this approach invites us to focus on the issues at hand rather than the people involved by placing the focus on how we are feeling and what we are thinking.
- For example, a teenager might say to a parent: "I feel frustrated when I'm always asked to spend more family time with you, because I would like to be able to hang out with my friends. In school, we really don't get to do that," versus "You always bug me. You don't understand. You never give me time to spend with my friends on the weekends."

- Consider which one is the better approach to resolution? Why might a resolution come about by using an I-statement?

4. Divide the participants into pairs. Ask one person to role-play the adult, the other to role-play the teenager. Refer the participants to the scenarios you listed on newsprint and give the pairs the option to choose one scenario. Now ask them to role-play the scenario using lots of "you statements."

After a few minutes, give a signal for the role-playing to cease, and ask the following questions:
- For those being confronted, how did the you-statements make you feel?
- For those doing the confronting, how did it feel to be giving you-statements? Is this the appropriate attitude for seeking resolution? Why or why not?
- Did any of you come to resolution? If yes, describe.

5. Invite the pairs to repeat the scenarios, but intentionally using I-statements instead. When finished, ask the preceding questions regarding the use of I-statements.

6. Share the following points in these or your own words:
- Conflict happens, even despite our best efforts. We're all human, and when conflict arises, we sometimes make mistakes, whether through our words, our actions, or by not showing respect to others when they disagree with us. Realizing this, we all need a way to make things right again.
- For the Christian leader, that's where forgiveness and reconciliation come to the forefront. Reconciliation, however, may not be something that can be achieved in every situation. For example, in the case of abuse, the situation may not be one where reconciliation can be achieved, though forgiveness can. Whether forgiveness is needed from another person, from God, or from ourselves, forgiveness is something that is within our control. It is something we can seek and offer, no matter what the situation may be.
- Jesus sought resolution with respect to others, allowing them the freedom to make the right choice. In the following Scripture passage, Jesus focuses on the issue at hand by challenging those who chose to condemn. Jesus offered forgiveness; he did not condemn.

7. Proclaim John 8:2–11. Allow a moment of silence to follow. Then ask these questions for silent reflection:
- Think about your own life for a moment. Have there been times when you've condemned someone? (Pause.) Have there been times when you've sought forgiveness from someone? times when you've offered forgiveness to someone, whether it was received or denied? (Pause.)
- Think about someone in your life right now that you need to forgive. Have you thought about how you might ask for forgiveness? What might be keeping you from resolving the hurt?

8. Give each person a small piece of blank paper and a pen or pencil. Announce that the closing activity will give the participants a chance to personalize everything they have heard about conflict resolution, and time to think about their own need to resolve conflict.

9. Ask the participants to think about a conflict in their life that has not been settled or one that ended badly. Tell them to write the name of the person involved on the small piece of paper and fold it as many times as they can.

10. Proclaim Matthew 5:23–24. Allow a few moments for reflection. Then read the passage a second time, and invite the participants to reflect on their thoughts and feelings.

11. Take the basket and pass it around the group. Tell the participants to put in the basket the paper they have been holding. Then offer the following comments:
- Resolving conflict is a sign of a mature leader. Christian leaders search for ways to resolve conflict, and know that in doing so they are leaving childish actions and attitudes behind.
- Resolving conflict is a sign of a courageous leader. Christian leaders are strong enough to patch up broken relationships and strong enough to break free from anger. Christian leaders are strong enough to risk being rejected. They are strong enough to move toward peace.
- Resolving conflict is a sign of a caring leader. When a Christian leader resolves a conflict with someone, they show that they care.
- Resolving conflict is a sign of freedom. Christian leaders free themselves from negative feelings, from wanting to hurt someone or get even, and from coming out on top by keeping others down.
- Resolving conflict is a sign of God's presence. God wants all of us to be reconcilers. Jesus gave his life to reconcile people with God. The Holy Spirit gives each of us the strength and wisdom to become reconcilers.

12. Ask one of the participants to hold up the basket as you conclude by praying the following prayer:
- Forgiving God, with your help we will let go of our grudges, hurts, and bad feelings caused by our conflicts with these people. With your help we will begin the process of reconciliation and healing, as you call us to do. We care about these people. And we know that they care about us. We ask for the courage to take the first step, in the name of Jesus, the healer. Amen.

Prayer of Sending Forth

Preparation

- Gather the following items:
  - ☐ a permanent marker
  - ☐ a small rock for each participant
  - ☐ *The Catholic Youth Bible* or another Bible
  - ☐ two bookmarks
  - ☐ a tape or CD player, and a recording of reflective instrumental music (optional)
- With a permanent marker, write each person's name on a rock. If you are unable to locate uniformly sized rocks for all, use one large rock and write everybody's name or initials on it.
- Recruit two volunteers to be readers. Set the Bible on a table and mark the following passages:
  + Matthew 16:18
  + Psalm 118:22

1. Gather the participants near the Bible. If you wish to use reflective instrumental music, begin playing it at this time.

2. Give each person the rock you prepared for her or him, or if you have decided to use a single rock, pass it around the group. Ask the participants to hold the rock, squeeze it, turn it over, look at its color, and feel its texture and weight. Tell them to notice how solid it is and how cool it is to their touch.

Invite the participants to suggest good uses of rocks. They may refer to the use of rocks as building materials, in fortifications, as gems, as decoration, and for sanding, buffing, drilling, and carving.

Then ask them to name some destructive uses of rocks. They may identify the use of rocks as weapons—thrown or catapulted as is, or carved into axes and pointed tools of warfare.

Ask the participants to keep all those ideas in mind as they listen to the scriptural readings that follow.

3. Signal the first reader to take the Bible from the table and proclaim Matthew 16:18. When the first reader finishes, tell him or her to give the Bible to the second reader. Instruct the second reader to proclaim Psalm 118:22.

4. Briefly identify the two scriptural images of rocks or stones as building materials: Jesus saw Peter as a rock-solid foundation for the Church, and the psalmist used the image of a rock to refer to God's strength. Ask the participants what rock-like qualities they as leaders have. Summarize with the following words:
  ○ We are all like rocks. It is good to be strong like a rock and to stand up for what we believe, no matter how hard we are being squeezed. But like rocks that bring destruction, we also hurt people by being hard and uncaring. We can be stubborn and refuse to budge. We can throw around attitudes and words just as we throw rocks. Our words can hit and hurt.

5. Ask the participants to close their eyes, inviting them into the following reflection:
- Think about someone who really hurt you by throwing words like rocks. Maybe they said something to you or something about you that hurt. Maybe they did not even try to see your side of something that was really important to you. Are you still close to that person? Have you resolved the problem? Have you forgiven that person? If you can, take a moment to tell God that you are ready to forgive that person.
- Now think of someone you hurt recently by throwing verbal rocks. Maybe you were hard-hearted or hardheaded. How did your words affect your relationship with that person? Have you resolved your problem? Have you apologized? If you can, take a moment to tell God that you are ready to ask for forgiveness.

6. Tell the participants to open their eyes. If you gave everyone their own rock, encourage them to take it home and to use it as a reminder of the importance of forgiveness and good conflict resolution. Suggest that they say a prayer for the people the rock represents for them, and that they apologize to the person they have hurt or forgive the person who has hurt them.

My Style

For each situation circle the letter that represents your first reaction.

1. It is Friday night. As usual your friends want to hang out at the mall and get a pizza. You are tired of doing the same old thing all the time, but you really like being with your friends. You . . .
   a. tell them that they are boring and that unless they do something a little more interesting, you are not going.
   b. go along with them because you like being with your friends, even though you are bored.
   c. plan to get your friends to make a list of all the possible things they could do together on Friday nights, decide which ones interest everybody, and do one each Friday night.
   d. suggest something new to do this Friday night and ask someone else to think up something for next Friday night.

2. Your younger brother borrowed your bike without asking. This is not the first time he has done this. You . . .
   a. yell at him and threaten him within an inch of his life.
   b. ask him why he likes using your bike better than using his own. If he has a good reason, you tell him that he can borrow your bike if he asks first.
   c. don't say anything to him but tell your parents.
   d. help him get his bike in good shape.

3. Your dad wants you to help him work in the yard and clean out the garage this Saturday. You have made plans with your friends, and you are looking forward to spending the day with them. You . . .
   a. say nothing about your plans to your dad and tell your friends that your dad wants you to stay home. Then you give your dad the silent treatment.
   b. tell your dad about your plans. Then you ask him if you can help him out on another day so that you can go with your friends.
   c. tell your dad about your plans. Then you ask him if you can go with your friends in the morning and help him in the afternoon.
   d. blow up at your dad.

4. A friend said something that really embarrassed you in front of a group of people at school. You . . .
   a. tell your friend that you did not like what happened and that you were embarrassed.
   b. look for a chance to do the same thing to your friend.
   c. talk to another friend about how upset you are with the person who embarrassed you.
   d. ask someone to tell your friend how upset you are.

Handout 2: Permission to reproduce is granted. © 2006 by Saint Mary's Press.

5. Your teacher has assigned you and two of your classmates to work on a science project that is due in three weeks. All three of you must do the project together, and one grade will be given. One person in your group is not doing her share of the work. You . . .
   a. try to do her work in addition to your own because you don't want to risk getting a bad grade.
   b. have a talk with her and the other person in your group. Together the three of you make a plan that works for everyone involved.
   c. blame her for not doing her part. You make sure she knows that you think she is dumb and lazy and that the project is behind schedule because of her.
   d. have a talk with her and offer to help her complete some of her assignment, but ask her to do the rest.

6. A friend has been ignoring you lately. She has been hanging around with a different group of girls and doing things you don't like. When you try to talk to her at school, she brushes you off. You . . .
   a. try to talk with her outside of school. You tell her how concerned you are about the things she has been doing with her new friends.
   b. hang around with her and her new group of friends once in a while.
   c. find a new group of friends.
   d. cuss her out and talk about her behind her back.

7. For about a year, you have been baby-sitting and doing odd jobs for a family. When you started, they agreed to pay you three dollars an hour. Lately they have been paying you less. You . . .
   a. try to find a job that pays well and refuse to work for this family as often.
   b. keep on working for them no matter what they pay you. After all, something is better than nothing.
   c. talk to them about the problem. Perhaps you can come up with a solution that is good for you and the family.
   d. quit working for them altogether. If anyone asks, you tell them how unfair the family was to you.

8. You are on a committee to plan an end-of-the-school-year party. You have some good ideas that are different from everyone else's. You are convinced that everyone would have a great time if the committee used your ideas. You . . .
   a. try to get at least one or two of your ideas worked into the final plan.
   b. disagree with the others' ideas, but do not argue because you are outnumbered.
   c. quit the committee and plan your own party for the same time.
   d. present your ideas to the group, listen to everybody's ideas, and try to come up with a plan that will be the most fun for everybody.

9. Your group of friends doesn't get along with another group in your grade. You know that one of these days, a fight will break out between the two. You . . .
   a. get ready to join in the fight when it happens.
   b. try to talk to some of the people in the other group and think about becoming friends with them.
   c. pretend there is no problem.
   d. encourage your group to talk to the other group.

10. Your teacher has asked for suggestions on how to spend the money your class made on a recent bike-a-thon. Your best friend has a good idea, but so do others. In fact, you like a few of your classmates' ideas better than you like your best friend's idea. When it comes to the final vote, you . . .
 a. vote for your friend's idea just to make him happy.
 b. vote for the idea you want, and explain to your friend why you did.
 c. don't vote.
 d. vote for the idea you want and then make sure your friend overhears you say to someone else that you didn't like any other ideas.

This chart can help you find your style of conflict resolution. Next to each number, circle the letter you chose. Count the number of circled letters in each column and write the total in the blank at the bottom. Your highest score indicates the way you most often deal with conflict. If two or three totals are the same, or if all four totals are close, you use a variety of styles.

Situation	Avoid	Work Against	Work Together	Meet Halfway
1	B	A	C	D
2	C	A	D	B
3	A	D	B	C
4	C	B	A	D
5	A	C	B	D
6	C	D	A	B
7	B	D	C	A
8	B	C	D	A
9	C	A	D	B
10	A	D	B	C

(The material on this handout is adapted from *Dealing with Tough Times,* by Marilyn Kielbasa [Winona, MN: Saint Mary's Press, 1999], page 52; and *Dealing with Tough Times* student workbook, pages 16–19. Copyright © 1999 by Saint Mary's Press. All rights reserved.)

The Mediation Process

Step 1: Telling the Story—Just the Facts

- Ask each party to tell honestly what happened.
- Listen to each party tell his or her version of what happened without interruption.

Step 2: Telling the Story—How the Parties Feel

- Ask the parties to share how they feel about what happened, and why.
- Ask each party if she or he understands why the other parties feel as they do.

Step 3: Brainstorming for Solutions

- Remind the parties that mediation is about finding a win-win solution that is fair to all parties.
- Ask all the parties to think of as many ways as possible to solve this conflict.

Step 4: Choosing the Best Solution

- Ask the parties which possible solutions they like best.
- Ask the parties which solutions they feel they can agree to.
- Make sure the solutions the parties agree to are realistic and doable.
- If all the parties can agree to one of the suggested solutions, declare the dispute settled. If all the parties cannot agree to one of the suggested solutions, declare that the dispute cannot be settled. The parties in an unresolved dispute now may look for another solution, or they may opt out of the mediation process and continue the conflict.

Step 5: Looking to the Future

- Ask the parties for ideas on how to prevent this conflict from happening again.

(This process is adapted from *Mediation: Getting to WinWin!* teacher's guide, by Fran Schmidt [Miami: Peace Education Foundation, 1994], pages 28–29. Copyright © 1994 by Grace Contrino Abrams Peace Education Foundation.)

Conflict Case Studies

Cut apart these case studies along the broken lines.

Curfew Conflict

The community of Marshall Heights is having problems with young people committing vandalism and fighting at night. Older people have been harassed. Property damage is occurring several times a week. The police have reported that groups of young people are roaming the streets in the evenings, and they believe these groups are the ones causing most of the problems.

The citizens of the town are insisting that the town board pass a curfew. The board is proposing a law to keep all young people under the age of seventeen off the streets after 9:00 p.m. on weekdays and after midnight on weekends.

Many young people are upset because they believe this law is unfair to the young people who do not cause trouble and that everyone is being punished for what a few are doing.

The town board has asked your group to mediate this dispute.

How do you proceed?

To Serve or Not to Serve

Parish policy is to not allow young people under the age of seventeen to serve as a lector, a Eucharistic minister, or a music or hospitality minister at the parish liturgies. The liturgy committee believes that young people are not mature enough to serve in these ministries. A group of parishioners strongly disagree with this policy and want it to be rescinded or revised so that no community members are excluded from serving at the liturgies.

The pastor has asked your group to help mediate this dispute.

How do you proceed?

Resource 3: Permission to reproduce is granted. © 2006 by Saint Mary's Press.

4 Trust-Based Leadership
Ready to Begin: Building Trust

Overview

Trust is foundational and necessary in all relationships. To accomplish anything, we must learn to work at trusting others and being trusted. Trusting others and being trusted by others is also necessary in leadership. One cannot be a leader without the participation and trust of others. This session will include activities and point to the Scriptures to teach how Jesus trusted others.

Preparation

- Gather the following items:
    - ☐ three decks of playing cards
    - ☐ a table
    - ☐ markers
    - ☐ masking tape
    - ☐ a blindfold
    - ☐ 100 or more thumbtacks, those with a round, flat head
    - ☐ a broom to sweep up the thumbtacks
    - ☐ newsprint
- Place the table in the middle of the room with a few cards already stacked and leaning together, to create the beginnings of a built-up structure.

1. As the young people arrive, give each of them the same number of cards and ask them to write their name on each card with a marker. Then give them directions to go over to the table and add to the structure. They must work together to allow one person at a time to place a card on the structure. If the structure or any of the cards fall, have each person collect the cards with their name on them and try to build a structure again. Allow 10 minutes for this activity.

2. Gather the participants and introduce the session by conducting a large-group discussion using the following questions:
- How important was each person's role in this activity?
- What did this activity teach us about trust and why trust is important for leadership?
- What role did a person's attitude play in this activity? What attitudes are needed to build trust?

3. Make the following points in your own words:
- Trust is foundational and necessary in all relationships. To accomplish anything, we must learn to work at trusting others and being trusted.

- Building a structure of cards required trusting everyone who participated. You trusted that the person placing a new card on the existing structure would be careful in their placement of the card and that they were taking their role seriously in accomplishing the building of the structure.
- Trusting others and being trusted by others is necessary in leadership. One cannot be a leader without the participation and trust of others.
- Accomplishments cannot be made unless others trust the leader and the leader trusts in others' abilities. In this session we will learn more about and build on the importance of trust in our relationships, especially in working together.

4. Ask for three pairs of volunteers. Ask these six participants to step outside the room for a moment. Once they are out of earshot, provide the remaining participants with the following directions:
- All of you will play an important role in this next activity. Three of the volunteers will be blindfolded and led through a maze by their partner, one at a time, by listening to the directions the partner shouts out to them.
- While each partner shouts out directions to lead his or her blindfolded partner through the maze, you all will shout out your own creative directions, some false and some truthful. At no time is anyone to touch the blindfolded volunteer. You can use only your voices; no movement among you should occur. Shout out directions only to the blindfolded volunteer on how to get through the supposed maze and no other information.

5. Make sure everyone understands their roles, and clarify if needed. Then place half the group on one side of where the trail will be and the other half on the other side of the trail. Place a piece of masking tape across the floor as a starting line. Then ask the first pair to come into the room and the brave volunteer to remove her or his shoes and socks and stand at the starting line. Ask the partner to stand among the rest of the group at either side.

6. Now toss the thumbtacks in a disarrayed fashion along what will be the trail, which should be approximately fifteen feet long. Tell the pair that one person will be blindfolded while the other will be led through the maze with the help of his or her trusted partner, though only through his or her voice. The partner is to shout out where the blindfolded volunteer should place his or her feet along the trail and in which direction he or she should turn, giving no information other than directions on where to step or move. Be sure that all understand, and inform them that you will shortly give a signal to begin.

7. Now blindfold the volunteer. Use a nonverbal symbol to ensure the group does not inform the blindfolded volunteer of what is about to happen. **Now sweep up the thumbtacks to remove them from the trail.** Be certain that all the thumbtacks have been picked up before proceeding. Now give the signal to begin.

Pay attention to the behavior of the group as the blindfolded volunteer is led through what she or he thinks is a trail of strewn thumbtacks. Have adult leaders record on newsprint what they observe in relation to working together and trust.

8. Once the first pair is finished, have them participate as a part of the crowd. Be sure to explain their new role. Now take pair number two through the process and then the remaining pair. When completed, have the group gather for discussion.

9. Ask the following questions in your own words:
   - (To the blindfolded volunteers) What went through your mind when you saw that you would be led through a trail of thumbtacks? Did you feel confident in trusting the partner you chose? What were the challenges of trying to listen to the voice of your trusted friend? Could you distinguish your friend's voice from the crowd? To which voices did you listen? Why?
   - (To the trusted partners) How did you feel about being in competition with the voices of the crowd shouting out false directions? Did you want to tell your friend that the thumbtacks were removed? How important was your role in this activity? How did it feel knowing that your friend had ultimate trust in you?
   - (To the crowd) What did you think when the thumbtacks were removed? Did you want to tell the brave volunteer they were removed? Did you like being in competition with the trusted friend, or did you want your friend's voice to be heard?

10. Now invite the participants to divide into groups of five or six people. Ask them to discuss the following questions:
- Why was trust important in this activity? Why is trust important in a relationship? Why is trust necessary in working together? Why is trust necessary in leadership?
- How would this activity have been different if Jesus was the trusted partner? Would you have known his voice?

Allow about 10 minutes for small-group discussion, and then invite each group to offer some input. Be sure the discussion includes the following points:
- To be trusted requires responsibility and commitment. If one fails at being trustworthy, the task at hand, or the relationship, can be negatively affected.
- As the trusted partner in this activity, Jesus would not have deceived his friend. He would have shouted, "Do not be afraid," to his friend, something he said many times to the people he met, letting them know that he could be trusted.
- We will listen to many voices when looking for direction in life. In the activity, you heard many different voices, some wanting to lead the blindfolded person in the wrong direction, some sounding believable and trustworthy. Like the trusted partners in the activity, Jesus is the one, true voice that leads us to goodness.
- Many of us struggle in trusting others. When someone says, "Trust me," few of us do. Most of us even think: "Oh yeah? You'll have to show me!" We want verifiable evidence that will cause our trust thermometers to rise. Trust building can be a major challenge.
- Other individuals are willing to trust without much prior or concurrent evidence. To become trustable, we must
  + build our credibility so others will respect us
  + keep confidences shared within our relationships
  + spend appropriate time together with those we are leading (or working with) so they know we're committed to the relationship

- follow through on our promises
- refrain from criticizing others
- respect others' boundaries
- admit our mistakes and take responsibility for correcting them
- always be honest

11. Conclude the session by asking the participants if they have any other suggestions for being a more "trustable" leader. Then invite the participants to join you in the prayer service, "Prayer of Sending Forth," at the end of this chapter.

Ready to Be Formed: Becoming Trustworthy

Overview

People must be able to trust a leader and the direction he or she gives. A leader who is not trusted loses effectiveness. Either the leader will be replaced or, if that is not an option, group members will move on. In this session the young people will participate in simulation exercises where working together and trusting the leader are essential to the tasks, and where the young people will assume responsibility for one another.

Preparation

- Gather the following items:
  - ☐ approximately 50 feet of rope or construction "caution" tape, to create the boundaries of an obstacle course
  - ☐ blindfolds, one for each participant
  - ☐ markers and newsprint
  - ☐ scissors, at least two pairs for each group of six to ten participants
  - ☐ glue sticks, at least two for each group of six to ten participants
  - ☐ various magazines, at least one for each participant
- You will need to prepare either an indoor or an outdoor obstacle course using the rope or caution tape and placing it in locations where the participants can climb under, climb over, or walk around them. Be sure to make safety your first priority, and make sure the course is in a location that cannot be viewed by the participants beforehand.
- Assign an adult leader to each small group of six to ten participants.

1. Gather the participants in a space separate from where the obstacle course is located. Divide the participants into even numbered groups of at least six and no more than ten. Have the groups stand in a circle facing one another. Then offer these directions:
  - Using your left hand, reach across and grab the hand of a person across from you. Consider your hands "super-glued," unable to become undone.
  - Now take your right hand and grab the hand of a different person within your circle. Consider these hands super-glued too.
  - The task of your group is to become untangled into either one or two interlocking circles. However, you cannot let go of one another's hands to do so. When you have completed the task, please sit as a group, remaining in your circle.

Ask the adult leaders to walk around to the different groups, observing only and making mental notes of what they observe in regard to leadership, communication, interdependence, and working together.

2. Gather the participants into a large group and conduct a discussion using these questions:
- What was difficult about accomplishing the task?
- Did any leaders come forth, or did your group share the leadership by everyone taking turns at giving direction?

- Who were the helpers of your group: those who offered an idea, some encouragement, or a bit of direction at some point during the activity? Why are helpers important, and how do they differ from the leaders?
- What role did communication play?
- What role did trust play, especially in those who served as leaders?

Now make the following points in your own words:
- Working together and sharing leadership takes time, yet everyone has ownership in the process of accomplishing the task; everyone's opinions and ideas are valued and accepted.
- Encouragement, help, and support are just as important and needed as direction. To function successfully a team needs to have a good balance of both. Leaders need to be attentive to creating this balance.
- Communication is key to understanding and working together. Communication means listening just as much as speaking.
- People must be able to trust a leader and the direction she or he gives. A leader who is not trusted loses effectiveness. Either the leader will be replaced or, if that is not an option, group members will move on. Our next activity will give us an experience of trusting leaders.

3. Ask the participants to form single-file lines of no more than eight people. Provide each participant with a blindfold and tell them that they are about to be led through an obstacle course blindfolded. Provide the following directions:
- Join hands with the person in front of you and the person behind you. Each of you will be asked to trust the person in front of you and to be responsible for the person behind you as you move through the obstacle course in your line. You will do this by telling the person behind you that you are responsible for his or her safety by saying that person's name, followed by, "I am responsible for your safety."

Have everyone follow suit, going down the line. Ask everyone to take their blindfolds and cover their eyes with it. Allow a few minutes for the participants to get their blindfolds situated. Now tell the group that the activity will take place in absolute silence. Remind them that they are responsible for the person behind them and that when the task is over, will be allowed to remove their blindfolds and talking can resume—but only then.

4. Once there is absolute silence, remove the blindfold of the first person in each line. Using a nonverbal signal, motion for the "leaders" to remain silent. Then motion for them to begin to lead their group through the obstacle course. Adult leaders should follow the group and remain close by to ensure safety, as well as to record what they observe.

5. When all lines have completed the obstacle course, invite all the participants to remove their blindfolds and ask all to be seated, creating a small group with the members of their assigned "line."

6. Distribute newsprint, markers, scissors, glue sticks, and magazines to each group. Ask them to work together, using good communication—both listening and speaking, and valuing each person's opinion—to create a display of what working together and trust in leadership means for them, based on this experience, as well as what they have learned. Allow about 10 to 15 minutes for the creation of the display, and allow for enough time for each small group to present its display to the entire group.

7. When small-group presentations are completed, summarize what you heard about working together and trust in leadership, noting this on newsprint. Feel free to expound on their points, being sure to include the following key points:

- Trusting and believing in a leader and his or her abilities is essential to succeeding.
- Sometimes we may be afraid that we will fall short on our responsibilities or we may fear that the leader will fail or that he or she is not leading in a way *we* think he or she should be leading.
- What can you as a leader do to nurture and develop trust in others? Surprisingly, the answer lies more in your own leadership behavior than it does in the behavior of your followers. Trust doesn't arise through demanding it. If you want trust, then you as leader must give it. You inspire trust by extending it.
- Trust emerges from acting responsibly, ethically, and consistently. The following six practices are key to your being trusted as a leader:
  + Tell the truth and live as your word. Trust that people not only want and deserve the truth but that they can handle it, warts and all. What they can't abide from a leader is any form of misinformation or deception, especially where promises are concerned.
  + You build your reputation for sincerity and reliability by keeping your word. When you realize you can't keep your word, for whatever reason, let your followers know immediately, and seek to renegotiate your promise.
  + Notice this principle does not say "Do not lie." The spirit of this practice is proactive, direct, open, sincere, and timely. Anything less is not worthy of you or them.
  + Listen . . . and keep listening. Once you have spoken what you honestly see or feel to be your truth, take a deep breath, pay strict attention, and keep completely silent while those around you voice their reaction. How you are seen to respond while listening either encourages further sharing of vital information or it closes down the possibility of frank exchange both now and in the future.
  + Admit mistakes publicly with the intent to learn. When you realize you've blown it or some brave soul brings this to your attention, admit your mistake immediately, and make sure you do whatever is needed to get back on track with the job and especially with the people involved.
  + Remember that others don't expect you to be perfect.

8. Conclude the session by leading the participants in the prayer service, "Prayer of Sending Forth," at the end of this chapter.

Ready to Be Empowered: Trust and Responsibility

Overview

Just as we must learn to trust others, one awesome realization is that God trusts us. Trust and responsibility go hand-in-hand. The Christian leader commits to living out this responsibility by taking action. This session will invite young people and their friends and families to do just that.

Preparation

- Gather the following items:
  - ☐ newsprint and markers
  - ☐ masking tape
- Determine which of the following activities will serve as the "core" of your session. Prepare and plan accordingly. The options include these:
  + *Plant trees.* Contact the National Arbor Foundation. Ask each of the young people and their families to contribute to the purchase of the trees (many types, appropriate to your zone, are inexpensive) and to help plant them in an appropriate and authorized predetermined area.
  + *Clean up your town or city.* Contact your town or city parks and recreation department, discussing the group's desire to help clean up and beautify the community and the possibility of scheduling a date and location for cleanup. Provide or ask the participants to come with rakes, trash bags, gloves, and so on, to clean up and beautify the chosen location.
- You will need to make prior arrangements with those in charge of the location as well as have parental permission forms filled out for transportation to and from the meeting place and the site. You will also need to coordinate the transportation.
- Post several sheets of newsprint on the wall in the gathering space and write the following question on it:
  + What does responsibility mean to you? What images, feelings, or words that you associate with responsibility come to mind?
- Send a letter home to invite the families and friends of the young people to participate in the activity.
- On a sheet of newsprint, list the following questions:
  + What did you learn today about responsibility?
  + How do we respond to the responsibility given to us by God with the resources we have?
  + How does it make you feel knowing that God trusts you with all that he has given us?
  + What are some other small ways you could be more responsible or responsive to God's trust in you?

1. As the participants gather, invite them to respond to the questions you have posted on the newsprint. They can do this either by writing their responses on the newsprint or by having them share their responses with one another. Once everyone has had the chance to respond to the questions, gather the group and introduce the activity by saying the following in your own words:

- Have you ever thought that trust and responsibility go hand in hand? Have you ever considered that God trusts you? It's true. God trusts us to be responsible not only with our own lives or with each other, but with all of creation.
- God doesn't leave us alone in that responsibility. God sends us the Holy Spirit to guide us in making the right decisions.
- God trusts us, because at the time of our creation, God placed the Holy Spirit within each of us. We were made in God's image and likeness, as told to us in the Book of Genesis. This sets us apart from any other creature or creation. Because of this we are given a responsibility like no other creature. That is because we are capable of caring for things and people in ways that no other creature is.
- Our relationship with God calls us to be in right relationship with other people. It doesn't matter whether those people are our best friends or our worst enemies. Our love for God must translate into a love for all people and all creation.
- We will be held accountable, not only for the things we do but also for the things we do not do.
- The Church provides us with teachings that are based on some key concepts that help guide and direct us toward greater responsibility to one another and to God. For example, we are called to respect and honor all life; we are called to treat all people with dignity and respect; and we are called to care for all of creation.
- An example of the problems our world faces today is the destruction of the environment, as seen with ozone-layer deterioration, pollution, and the loss of the rain forest.
- With the rise in urban and suburban construction, we see the loss of animal habitats and we suffer from the careless use of global resources, such as oil, gasoline, and clean water.
- So, how do we respond to such destruction? How do we take on the responsibility God has entrusted to us? We're going to answer those questions in this session.

2. Continue the session by explaining to the participants the activity they will conduct. Offer whatever specifics are needed, and be sure to check and see if there are any additional questions or concerns. Then implement the option you have preselected (planting trees or conducting a neighborhood cleanup).

3. Once you have completed the chosen learning activity, regather the participants and divide them into small groups of six people. If families are participating in the session, be sure the groups include the various generations.

Ask the small groups to consider the questions you have posted on the newsprint.

Allow 15 to 20 minutes for small-group discussion, and then invite the groups to share a few of their responses with the larger group.

4. Conclude by sharing your own experience and observations. Be sure to include these key points:
- Being a Christian leader means accepting the responsibility given us by God to care for the earth, its creatures, and its people; it is important to realize that this

responsibility is given to and shared by every human being. Everyone is called to act on that responsibility.
- The Christian leader takes this responsibility seriously, and is *consciously* concerned with and rooted in the mission of Jesus.
- Christian leadership is not just about leading meetings and organizing activities. Christian leadership involves the attitudes, motivations, and intentions of the person.
- How we live our lives is a true testament to what we believe. Living our faith *is* Christian leadership; therefore, taking on the responsibility of caring for the earth is Christian leadership in action—it is living and not just a mere concept.

5. Conclude the session by leading the participants in the prayer service, "Prayer of Sending Forth," at the end of this chapter.

Prayer of Sending Forth

Preparation

- Gather the following items:
  - ☐ red, orange, green, purple, yellow, blue, and red strips of construction paper, one for each participant
  - ☐ one copy of resource 4, "Rainbow Reading"
- Recruit a volunteer to proclaim 1 Corinthians 12:12–26 as it appears on resource 4.

1. Invite the participants to join you in a space for prayer, sitting closely in a group and facing front. Ask the group to quiet their bodies, minds, and hearts to recognize God's presence within and around them.

2. Begin by inviting the participants to make the sign of the cross by saying: "In the name of the Father, and of the Son, and of the Holy Spirit. Amen." Then offer the following opening prayer:
- Lord of all, you place your trust in us to bless and honor the different gifts and uniqueness of each individual, to care for one another and all your creation, and to follow the example of Jesus in leading your people to a greater experience of your love. Send us your Holy Spirit to guide us in our leadership and to enliven our sense of responsibility in this world so that we may act according to your will.
- Lord, help us to accept each other's differences and to see them as gifts from you that have a true purpose. May we come to realize the joy that comes from doing your will together. We ask this through Christ, our Lord. Amen.

3. Randomly distribute the colored strips of paper, and introduce the proclamation of Scripture in the following way:
- We are going to experience the Scriptures in a different way through everyone's participation. Whenever the word *rainbow* is said, everyone will lift their colored paper strip in the air and flap it for a moment. When you hear your specific color mentioned, you will do the same.
- Let us take a moment to prepare our hearts to hear and receive God's word through an adaptation of the first letter of Paul to the Corinthians (1 Cor. 12:12–26).

Ask the young person recruited earlier to proclaim the scriptural adaptation on resource 4. Follow with a brief moment of silence for personal reflection.

4. Invite those assembled to share and make the connection between what they just heard in the scriptural adaptation to what they experienced earlier through the learning activity.

5. Conclude by asking the participants to form one large circle and pray together to praise the gift of Jesus and for the intercession of Mary, mother of us all, through the Hail Mary.

6. End the session with any last-minute announcements. Refreshments may be served at this time.

Rainbow Reading

A reading from the first letter of Paul to the Corinthians.

The *rainbow* is one and has many colors, but all the colors, many though they are, are one *rainbow*; and so it is with Christ. It was in one Spirit that all of us, whether *red* or *yellow, purple* or *green*, were baptized into one *rainbow*. All of us have been given to drink of the one Spirit. Now the *rainbow* is not one color, but many. If *orange* should say, "Because I am not *blue* I do not belong to them," would it then no longer belong to the *rainbow?* If *green* should say, "Because I am not *red* I do not belong to the *rainbow*," would it no longer belong to them? If the *rainbow* were *purple*, what would happen to *yellow?* If it were *orange,* what would happen to *blue?* As it is, God set each color of the *rainbow* in the place God wanted it to be. If all the colors were alike, where would the *rainbow* be? There are indeed many different colors, but one *rainbow*. *Purple* cannot say to *yellow,* "I do not need you," any more than *red* can say to *blue,* "I do not need you." Even those colors of the *rainbow* that seem less important are in fact indispensable. If one color suffers, all the colors suffer with it; if one color is honored; all the colors share its joy. (Adapted from 1 Corinthians 12:12–26)

5 Leadership and Discipleship
Ready to Begin: Models of Discipleship

Overview

The things we value most, as well as our own strengths and personality traits, help to shape the way we lead. Through the example we set, we have the potential to influence the lives of those around us—their thoughts, feelings, and actions; so we can say that our leadership shapes the world around us.

This session invites the participants to identify and further reflect on their strengths and personalities, uniting them to a sense of purpose. The session is designed to serve as an invitation for personal reflection and connection with Jesus and his mission.

Preparation

- Gather the following items:
    - ☐ unlined paper
    - ☐ pencils with erasers, one for each participant
    - ☐ several pairs of scissors
    - ☐ Popsicle sticks, one for each participant
    - ☐ several glue sticks
    - ☐ crayons
    - ☐ newsprint and markers
    - ☐ legal-sized pieces of paper, one for each participant
    - ☐ pens, one for each participant
- Post the following questions on newsprint:
    + What trait, value, or practice would make you a better leader?
    + What trait, value, or practice will help you to better connect with God and become a better reflection of God in the world?

1. Gather the participants and distribute the unlined paper, pencils, Popsicle sticks, glue sticks, crayons, and scissors. Then offer the following comments in your own words:

- In this activity you will be asked to identify some of your strengths, things you're good at, the positive things you're known for, and some of the distinct personality traits that make you unique and the person you are.
- In thinking about your traits and strengths, and your uniqueness, think about what jungle or zoo animals best identify those traits? The task is to create a puppet using the characteristics of various animals that best symbolize the traits and strengths you possess. For example, you might choose the head of a lion if you are a person who is very vocal, the long neck of a giraffe if you are someone who sticks your neck out to help others, or the ears of an elephant because you are a good listener.

- Once you've selected the animals that display, or compare to, your own traits and such, draw the animals' features on the paper provided, cut them out, and glue them to the Popsicle stick to create a Popsicle stick puppet.
- Remember to be as creative as you can and have fun with the activity, but to remain true to the person you are in selecting your animals and what they represent in you.

Allow for 15 minutes of creativity and construction, and then call the participants together to share their puppets. You may choose to do this either in a large group or in smaller groups.

2. Following the presentations, make the following points in your own words:
- By identifying our strengths and unique personality traits, we can come to a better understanding of the roles we play and the kind of leadership we offer. For example, if you demonstrated reaching out to others by choosing the arms of a monkey or a koala bear, you've identified that reaching out to others is one way you set an example for others through your leadership. Reaching out to others is a value of yours.
- Let's take a moment to list on newsprint some of the traits and strengths that we heard shared. These are some of the ways each of you sets an example for others through your leadership.

3. Invite the participants to call out some values as you note them on the newsprint. Then continue with the next question:
- Now think about some of Jesus's strengths and personality traits. **For example**, Jesus liked to be with people, to hang out with them and share a meal with them. Jesus valued being with and present to people. What other values can we identify for Jesus?

Invite the participants to call out some values as you note them on the newsprint. Then continue:
- Let's look at some of the similarities we see from the two lists we generated.

Review both lists and note the similarities between the two. Then continue with your comments along this line:
- The things we value most, as well as our own strengths and personality traits, help to shape the way we lead. Through the example we set, we have the potential to influence the lives of those around us—their thoughts, feelings, and actions; so we can say that our leadership shapes the world around us.

4. Ask the participants to divide into smaller groups of five and to sit in a circle with their small-group members. Distribute the legal-sized paper and a pen to each participant. Introduce the activity with the following comments:
- A fundamental part of Christian leadership is discipleship.
- Discipleship is a commitment to learning from and following Jesus's teachings and example. It is a willingness to be led by Jesus.
- Each of us can identify people who have influenced our lives. They are the people we've learned from, whose example we've followed.
- Every leader is a teacher, and leaders leave behind a legacy (something that has been handed down), or their mark, in the world.
- Take a few moments to share in your small group some of the greatest leaders you know or know of, their legacies, and the marks they have left in the world.

Allow about 10 minutes for the groups to share. Then proceed with these comments:
- Now think about your own personal life. What people in your life have been your greatest teachers? What people have been the role models who have taught you about God, how to play fairly, how to become responsible, and how to make good choices? Take a few moments to share about them in your small group.

Allow about 10 minutes for the groups to share. Then proceed with these comments:
- Take your piece of paper and place it horizontally. Draw one horizontal line in the center of the paper, from one end to the other. In the center of the line, write the word *NOW* in capital letters (you may want to demonstrate using a sheet of newsprint).
- We've talked briefly about some of the greatest leaders we've come to know and what they have taught us. Take about 5 minutes and create a list of the people in your life by writing their names and the times they were present to you. Begin with the time of your birth and continue to the present time, being sure not to go beyond the word *NOW* on your paper.

You may wish to give an example from your own life to assure the participants understand the activity.

5. When everyone seems to be finished, ask the participants to share highlights from their lists within their small groups. After some sharing, make the following points for personal reflection:
- Now, think about the people you are leading, those for whom you set an example.
- Just as we've followed the leadership of Jesus, the saints, and our grandparents, parents, older siblings, teachers, coaches, friends, and other significant people in our lives, there are those who look to us for an example of how to live, act, love, and make right choices.
- Take a few minutes to identify those people in your life who look to you for your leadership, those who follow your example. Then place their names on your paper starting at the word *NOW* and continuing to the end of the right side of the paper.
- When finished, share about these people you've identified in your small groups and what you may be teaching them—or would like to start teaching them—through your example and leadership.

6. Conclude this segment by making the following points in your own words:
- For those of us who are Christians, the ultimate leader is Jesus. Jesus teaches us how to be happy and how to live life fully by following Gospel values: to love one another, to forgive those who wrong us, to put God at the center of our lives through prayer and worship, and to serve poor people, to name a few.
- Who were Jesus's teachers? Whose leadership did Jesus follow? What do you think these people taught Jesus? (A few examples are Joseph and Mary, John the Baptist, and Jesus's faith community.)
- Who has Jesus influenced by his leadership? What, do you think, are some of the key teachings of Jesus for young people today?

- Being happy and living life fully does not mean that life is ever easy. With life come disappointment and suffering and heartache. No one is immune to that—not even Jesus—but he teaches us what to do and how to live through those times all throughout the Gospels:
  + In the calming of the storm when the Apostles were frightened for their lives, Jesus taught them about having a little more faith and trust in him; Jesus taught them about the power of his presence and his love and care for them. Jesus taught them that even when we do not feel him near, he is never distant from us.
  + In the Garden of Gethsemane, right before Jesus was taken away by the guards, which began the road to his suffering and death on the cross, in his moment of utter despair, Jesus turned to God in prayer, and Luke's Gospel tells us he was comforted by an angel.
- Jesus taught us that whenever life challenges us or brings about suffering and pain, confusion, or questioning as to why bad things are happening, he is there in the midst of it all, never leaving us alone in it. Jesus taught us to turn to God in those most difficult moments—that not all is lost, even though it might feel that way.
- In following Jesus's leadership, we too can leave a powerful legacy, one that could transform the hearts of people to bring about peace, unity, and harmony, where there is no more war or no one has to go another day without food. All this begins with you and me. It begins by the way we live and share our lives with others, by the leadership and example we provide as well as the discipleship we model.

7. Ask the participants to consider their Popsicle stick puppets by reflecting on the questions you have posted on the newsprint for discussion within their small groups. Allow about 10 minutes for discussion.

8. Wrap up by making the following points in your own words:
- The personality traits, personal strengths, and talents given to us by God are the very tools needed to build the Kingdom of God here on earth.
- Each of us has a purpose in life, and every person created by God is called to love and to put that love into action, whether that person is Christian or non-Christian.
- Because of our intrinsic goodness, each of us has the ability to lead by example. Through our leadership and discipleship, we share in the mission of Jesus with conviction.
- Jesus is the king of heaven and earth, the head of the Church. Through our Baptism we are connected to him and to his mission. The mission of the Church is the mission of Jesus: to clothe the naked, feed the hungry, serve the poor, love one another, and worship God. Reflect on your gifts, traits, and strengths. What is your place among the Church? How can you use what you've been given to better the Church and build it up?

9. Conclude the session by leading the participants in the prayer service, "Prayer of Sending Forth," at the end of this chapter.

Leadership and Discipleship

Ready to Be Formed: Servant Leadership

Overview

Leadership for Jesus, and for the Christian, is about being a servant. It is not having arrived at a place of prominence; it is having humbled oneself to a place of solidarity with the poor and compassionate love in action. This session will seek to develop and call the participants to this philosophy as a way of life. Unlike other sessions, this one is outlined for a half-day session and will include going off-site.

Preparation

- Gather the following items:
  - ☐ one small bag of balloons
  - ☐ items needed based on the activity of service selected
  - ☐ large-sized index cards, five or six for each small group of five people
  - ☐ markers
- Place one chair for each team (of five people) at the opposite end of the room, and put a balloon on each chair.
- Select and coordinate the involvement of the young people in an already ongoing activity of service coordinated by your parish, or coordinate an activity of service in conjunction with the social justice or outreach ministry within your parish. If neither is available, these are some other suggestions:
  + Serve at a local soup kitchen.
  + Visit the elderly at a local nursing home and organize games and activities in which to participate with them.
  + Volunteer to work at a local food bank.

1. Gather the participants and introduce the activity by making the following points:
  ○ Working together takes time, and working interdependently is what being a member of the Body of Christ is all about.
  ○ Interdependence means calling forth the needed gifts and abilities in others to use for the good of all. Interdependence understands that certain gifts are needed some of the time, but not necessarily all the time.
  ○ Interdependence understands that not everyone has the same gifts to share and that everyone is needed at some point to offer their gifts and abilities.
  ○ Interdependence is not about competition. It honors, respects, and values all members.
  ○ For this first activity, you will have to function interdependently. Each of you will be assigned a different ability, yet the task is to work together, interdependently and as one unit—one body.

2. Divide the participants into teams of five, asking the teams to assign two of their team members to be the legs of the body, one person the hands, one the mouth, and one the "gluteus maximus." Once the parts have been assigned, explain the following:

73

- (Ask the legs to step forward.) Legs are used for walking, for helping us get from one place to another. This is your one and only function. Legs do not talk. They do not lift or grasp anything. They do not act in any other way but to walk and to serve as the legs for the team.
- (Ask the hands to step forward.) Hands are used for grasping and holding, carrying and lifting. This is your only function. Hands do not talk. They do not walk or function in any other way but to serve as hands for the team.
- (Ask the mouth to step forward.) The mouth is used to taste, to take air in and to blow it out. Mouths are used for talking. They are not to walk, grasp, lift or carry anything or to function in any other way but to serve as the mouth for the team.
- (Ask the gluteus maximus to step forward.) The gluteus maximus is for sitting. It provides cushion for the body. The gluteus maximus does not talk, but it does make noises from time to time. It does not walk, carry or hold anything, or function in any other way but to serve as the gluteus maximus for the team.
- As of right now, you are to function only in the ways just described, according to the body part you've been assigned. Remember, only the mouths can talk.
- The object of the game is to work together, interdependently, to get from one side of the room to the chair on the other side of the room, where a balloon is waiting to be blown up and popped.
- Once your team has successfully functioned as one body and has popped your balloon, return to the starting point, functioning still as your assigned body part, where the race ends.

Be careful not to give the group any time to plan and talk through how they will complete the task. Ask them to raise their hands if any of the directions need to be clarified. When ready, give them a signal to begin.

3. Regather the participants and ask the following questions:
- What was the experience like?
- Which parts of the body were most important?
- Which parts played less of a role? What does this activity teach about people whose gifts and talents may not be those needed for a particular task?
- Why should they be as equally honored as those whose gifts and talents are needed more often?

4. Invite the participants to divide into small groups of six to eight people. Provide each group with a few index cards and a marker or two. Ask them to respond to the following questions by noting their answers on the cards provided:
- What words or images come to mind when you hear the word *leader*?
- What words or images come to mind when you hear the word *servant*?

Once the groups have had a few minutes to write down their answers, repeat each question, asking them to hold up their cards to show their responses. Ask everyone to take a good look at the responses. If you'd like, you may even post the cards on a nearby wall for better viewing.

Make the following points in your own words:
- A servant is not a slave. A servant works to build up, to affirm, to encourage, to invite, to forgive, to love, and to respect others.

- Jesus was the ultimate servant leader. He did not flaunt his power or that he was the Son of God; instead he humbled himself and focused on loving others. He healed and cured people because of love. He calmed fears because of love. He hung out with the outcasts because of love. He suffered and died on a cross because of love. He rose from the dead and offers us eternal life because of love. Jesus went beyond himself because of love. He calls us to do the same.
- Jesus taught us how to be servant leaders by how he lived. One story from the Scriptures that beautifully displays this is "Jesus Washes the Disciples' Feet," where Jesus, at the Last Supper, ties a towel around his waist, bends to his knees, and washes the disciples' feet. No worldly king would have done anything like this for anyone in his kingdom, but Jesus did. He tells us that the greatest among us are not the ones who have positions of authority, money, or fame. The greatest among us are the ones who serve (Luke 22:24–27).
- What we know, through the example Jesus gives us in this story, is that serving others is central to being a disciple of Jesus. Listen attentively as we hear this story from John's Gospel.

Proclaim John 13:1–15, "Jesus Washes the Disciples' Feet," as a lead-in to the introduction of the service activity. Invite the participants, using these or similar words:
- Now, just as we've been given the example, let us go forth and do the same.

5. Introduce the activity of service you have preselected. Be sure to provide all the necessary specifics regarding the project. Make sure no questions or clarifications are needed. Then depart. (Depending on the activity selected, it should happen within a 2- to 3-hour time frame.)

6. Upon return, regather the participants and ask the following questions for large- or small-group discussion:
- What does this activity of service have to teach us about servant leadership?
- Why do you think service is important in the life of a disciple of Jesus?
- Should service be "something we do," or are we called to adopt it as a way of life? What is the difference?

Wrap up the discussion by adding the following points and focusing on the questions for large-group discussion to generate and identify some concrete ideas for adopting a way of service for the participants' lives:
- Serving others doesn't always necessitate an event. Serving others can also happen in simple ways, like helping a friend, offering a kind smile, volunteering a few hours of your time, helping your parents around the house, and so on. What simple ways of service could you adopt in your daily life?
- Service, for the Christian, is not about doing something for others every once in a while; service is a way of life. We see this in the way Jesus lived his life. Whenever he found a person in need, Jesus reached out to him or her.
- What are some of the ordinary situations you encounter in which your presence, kindness, resources, skills, and gifts could benefit others?
- Servant leadership invites us to become aware of the needs of others and to respond to those needs in simple and ordinary ways.

7. Conclude the session by leading the participants in the prayer service, "Prayer of Sending Forth," at the end of this chapter.

Ready to Be Empowered: Discipleship Rooted in Christ

Overview

In the Scriptures we find numerous examples of how Jesus rooted himself in the mission of his Father. After Jesus's Resurrection the disciples rooted their mission in the life and message of Christ. In this session the participants will explore how Christian leadership and discipleship are rooted in the life of Jesus.

Preparation

- Gather the following items:
  - ☐ newsprint
  - ☐ a copy of *The Tree that Survived the Winter,* by Mary Fahy (Mahwah, NJ: Paulist Press, 1989)
  - ☐ a variety of colored markers
  - ☐ unlined paper
  - ☐ cutouts of a variety of trees that bear fruit, such as apples, bananas, peaches, grapefruit, and so on
  - ☐ thumbtacks
  - ☐ a large wooden cross and its stand
- Write the gifts of the Holy Spirit on newsprint: wisdom, understanding, right judgment, courage, knowledge, reverence, and wonder and awe.
- Write the fruits of the Holy Spirit on newsprint: charity, joy, peace, patience, goodness, kindness, faithfulness, long-suffering, humility, modesty, continence, and chastity.

1. Gather the participants and introduce the session by making the following points in your own words:
  - Through our Baptism, we become a part of Christ's Body, the Church. This means we enter into Jesus' very life—the joys, blessings, and graces—as well as into his suffering, death, and Resurrection. Because Jesus entered into our humanity, there is no pain or joy he does not know. No matter what we experience in life, we are never alone. Jesus is a part of all of it, and so are the many others who make up Christ's Body with us. Because of this oneness in Christ, we share in the one faith, one Baptism, and one suffering, death, and resurrection.
  - Living a life of faith has its mountaintop experiences and its bottom-of-the-well experiences too. There are times when, like Peter, we want to build tents and stay on the mountaintop in the story of the Transfiguration of Jesus (Matt. 17:1–13), when we don't want to leave the experience of God's presence, such as after a powerful retreat. There are also times when we feel abandoned and wonder where God is, just like Jesus experienced when he was on the cross and cried out to God the Father, "My God, my God, why have you forsaken me?" (Mark 15:34).

- We are about to hear a story about a tree who grows in God's warmth and love, but who also wonders where God is when she experiences the death of fall and winter.
- Just as the tree experiences seasons in her life of suffering, death, and resurrection, so do we.
- What makes the life of a disciple unique is that we share in the life of Jesus and in his mission. We follow his teachings and his leadership as we journey through our lives toward a deeper relationship with him.
- As you listen to the story, see if you can identify with any of the thoughts and feelings the tree has in her life, as she goes through the fall and winter into spring. See too if any of the tree's experiences were like those of Jesus.

2. Read *The Tree that Survived the Winter.* Follow with a brief sharing in the large group by asking these questions:
- What are some of the similarities between the experiences of the tree and your own life experiences? For example, has there ever been a time in your life when you felt so alive or when you felt as if you'd survived a particular experience, like a semester of a subject in school with which you struggled?
- What are some of the similarities between these and the life of Jesus? Were there times when he felt alone and abandoned by God? (Remind them of the Crucifixion, where Jesus cried out in a loud voice, "My God, my God, why have you forsaken me?" [Mark 15:34].)

3. Have the participants gather in small groups at tables. Distribute the plain paper and colored markers and ask the participants to use up the entire paper to draw a tree, symbolizing themselves, with a strong root system. Have them focus on drawing only the trunk, branches, and root system for now. Allow a minute or two for them to draw, and then ask the following in your own words:
- Being a disciple means being rooted in Christ. Take a moment to look at the strong root system you've drawn and to answer the question, "Who and what has nourished my growth in being rooted in Christ?"
- Write the names of the people, experiences, and values on your root system. For example, you might write your grandmother's name, the date of your Baptism, or that you value honesty. When finished, share your root system with your small group.

Allow about 10 minutes for the participants to complete the task and to share their responses in small groups.

4. Now ask the participants to focus on the top part of the tree: its branches. Ask them to consider what helps them reach upward toward God in prayer and in living the Gospel values. Ask them also to consider what ways they reach out to others. Have them jot down their answers on the branches of the tree. For example: with music, during alone time, by having friends who value the same things, by going to Mass. When finished, invite the participants to share their branches within their small groups.

5. Distribute the cutouts of the different varieties of fruit and make the following points in your own words:
- The story of Creation tells us that we were created good, and that this goodness, along with many gifts, comes from God. We come to know this through the Holy Spirit and the seven gifts given when we receive the Holy

Spirit in his fullness at Confirmation. (Refer to that which you've outlined on the newsprint.) These seven gifts are wisdom, understanding, right judgment, courage, knowledge, reverence, and wonder and awe (Isa. 11:2–3).

Ask the participants to define each of the gifts or offer examples of each gift. The following information can be shared if they get a bit stuck:

- *Wisdom.* Through wisdom, the wonders of nature, every event in history, and all the ups and downs of our lives take on deeper meaning and purpose.
- *Understanding.* The gift of understanding is the ability to comprehend how a person must live his or her life as a follower of Jesus.
- *Right judgment.* The gift of right judgment is the ability to know the difference between right and wrong and then to choose what is good.
- *Courage.* The gift of courage enables us to take risks and to overcome fear as we try to live out the Gospel of Jesus.
- *Knowledge.* The gift of knowledge is the ability to comprehend the basic meaning and message of Jesus Christ.
- *Reverence.* Sometimes called piety, the gift of reverence gives the Christian a deep sense of respect for God.
- *Wonder and awe.* The gift of wonder and awe in the presence of God is sometimes translated as "the fear of the Lord." Though we can approach God with the trust of little children, we are also often aware of God's total majesty, unlimited power, and desire for justice.
  - We can create goodness through our actions and choices: we can love, we can be kind, and we can create peace. These are further outlined in the Scriptures as the fruits of the Holy Spirit. They are charity, joy, peace, patience, goodness, kindness, faithfulness, long-suffering, humility, modesty, continence, and chastity.

Again, ask the participants to offer definitions or examples of each of the fruits.

6. Now ask the participants to consider the fruits of their actions and choices and to print them clearly on the fruit cutouts. For example, a fruit in their life may be kindness, because they make a conscious effort to help people even when they may not have the time or the desire. Another may be gentleness because they are able to reflect God as one who loves everybody by their effort to respect others' ideas and beliefs. Ask them to write what their fruit is, as well as why it is a fruit in their lives. Tell them that they need not stick only to the fruits of the Holy Spirit, but may include any fruit or goodness that has come about because of their actions and choices.

7. While the participants identify the fruits of their labors, set up the large cross in the center of the space. When the participants are finished, share the following in your own words:

- We began our session by hearing the story of a tree and the trials she faced. These same trials are common in our own lives. Being a disciple of Jesus leads us to the cross, yet we know that it is not a tree of death; rather it is the tree of life.
- The cross, our sufferings or trials in life, leads us to growth, just like the tree who survived winter and all she experienced. Spring, resurrection, awaits each one of us, and the goodness of the cross is made known through our lives. The people in our lives come to know its goodness through the fruits of our lives.

Leadership and Discipleship

- Each of you has taken the time to reflect on the fruits of your lives, the goodness you've created and shared with others. As young disciples of Christ, I'd like to invite each of you, one by one, to come forward and tack your fruits to the cross as a symbol of the goodness and life promised to each of us when we root our lives in Christ.

8. Review the fruits by reading them aloud to the group; conclude by making the following points in your own words:
- Because of God's action in our lives, we reflect who God truly is by the way we live through the Holy Spirit. When we live out our goodness, we create more goodness with God—we cocreate with God.
- This is the life of the disciple—one who connects with God to bring about the fullness and goodness of life, even when it is tough and we don't feel like it, or when we don't feel that what we do can make a difference.
- We see this in the person of Jesus. He took time to go off by himself to connect with God the Father through prayer. It was because of this connection that Jesus gained the strength to persevere through some of the tough times in his life, like when his friend Lazarus died, when he was frustrated with the Apostles because they just didn't "get it," or when he suffered along the road to Calvary.
- Sometimes we think that to make a difference, it has to be a big event or action. Jesus taught us that we don't have to part the Red Sea to make a difference. He showed us that the important differences we can make are in the lives of the people we meet, simply by forgiving them, loving them, accepting them, listening to them, and including them.
- Just like in the story of the woman caught in adultery who was almost stoned to death, Jesus told her that he didn't come to condemn her; rather he forgave her (John 8:2–11). Although he didn't part the Red Sea in this case, it had the same effect. It freed her. We can do the same, for others and for ourselves, but not without the help of God by connecting with him through our own prayer.
- Just as in the title of the old tune *They'll Know We Are Christians by Our Love* (Peter Scholtes, F.E.L. Publications, 1966), disciples of Jesus are known by their fruits—the fruit of their actions, thoughts, and leadership.

9. Conclude the session by leading the participants in prayer using the prayer service, "Prayer of Sending Forth," at the end of this chapter.

Prayer of Sending Forth

Preparation

- Gather the following items:
  - ☐ four copies of *The Catholic Youth Bible* or another Bible
  - ☐ colored beads in red, orange, yellow, pink, green, blue, purple, and brown, approximately three times the number of the group (in other words, if the group size is twenty, you will need approximately sixty beads of each color)
  - ☐ eight small bags or containers for beads
  - ☐ twine, one six- to eight-inch piece for each participant, for bracelets
  - ☐ songbooks or hymnals
  - ☐ a prayer table
  - ☐ a small cross
  - ☐ a candle
  - ☐ newsprint and a marker
  - ☐ CDs of reflective instrumental music and a CD player
  - ☐ unlined paper, one piece for each participant
  - ☐ pens and pencils
- Prepare three or four young people to proclaim 1 Corinthians 12:12–26 by dividing the reading into sections and providing each reader with a Bible.
- Separate the colored beads into separate bags for easy selection. Cut up the twine as indicated.
- Invite some of the young people to lead, either vocally or instrumentally, the song that is selected to conclude the prayer.
- Create a prayer space. Include a prayer table, the bags of colored beads, the twine, an open Bible, a small cross, and a candle.
- Post the following on newsprint:
  + red = unconditional love
  + orange = enthusiasm
  + yellow = kindness
  + pink = joy
  + green = encouragement
  + blue = peace
  + purple = faith
  + brown = leadership
- Choose a closing song such as *Somos el Cuerpo de Cristo/We Are the Body of Christ*, by Jaime Cortez; *One Bread, One Body*, by John Foley; *Song of the Body of Christ*, by David Haas; or another song on the theme of discipleship.

1. Invite the group to join you in the prayer space. Ask them to make a circle around the prayer table. Play some quiet instrumental music and invite the group to quiet their bodies, minds, and hearts to recognize God's presence within and around them. Now begin with the sign of the cross: "In the name of the Father, and of the Son, and of the Holy Spirit. Amen."

2. Say the following:
- Let us now prepare our hearts to listen to God's word through the Scripture reading from Paul's first letter to the Church in Corinth, where he tells them about the importance of the gifts each person is given to share.

Invite the prepared young people to proclaim 1 Corinthians 12:12–26. Allow for a brief moment of silence to follow.

3. Offer the following comments:
- Leadership is not always easy.
- Paul reminds us that although we are very different, each one of us is needed for what we have to offer, and that together we are the one Body in Christ.
- Jesus is the ultimate leader from whom we can learn and receive ultimate direction. We are connected to him, to his life and his mission, through our Baptism. We share in his life and mission, and he depends on us to continue to reflect his love by washing each other's feet in adopting service as a way of life. Each of us is needed and depended on to share all that we have been given to build up the Kingdom here on earth.
- What we are about to do is called affirmation, which is naming and honoring a particular gift we have come to experience through someone.
- In our time together, we have come to experience many fine qualities and attributes in one another. We've experienced that some people bring a real sense of peace or calm to a group. The enthusiasm of others has motivated the work and participation of the group. And the shared faith of still others has inspired us and caused us to reach toward God a little bit more.

4. Provide a piece of paper and a pen or pencil to each individual, asking them to write their name on it. Distribute one piece of twine to each person, as well as the bags of separated beads, asking each person to place a small pile of five or six beads of each color in front of them. When everyone is ready, ask each of the participants to pass their piece of twine placed on top of the paper with their name written on it to the person to their right. Everyone should be holding the name and piece of twine of the person to their left. Ask everyone to reflect on the different qualities they have experienced in this person and invite them to choose the color bead that corresponds to the quality they see in that person and thread the bead onto the twine. Use the bead chart to help the group identify qualities. When finished, give a signal for the entire group to move the name and piece of twine they have to the person on their right. Continue until the pieces of twine have completed the circle and everyone has the paper with their name on it and their piece of twine in front of them, now donned with beads.

Note: If you have a rather large group (more than twenty), you may wish to divide the large group into smaller groups to decrease the amount of time this step will take.

5. Allow a few moments of silence for the participants to reflect on the affirmations of the entire group. Following this, gather the group into one large circle and pray together in the words Jesus taught us: "Our Father . . ."

6. Conclude the prayer time by providing the participants with songbooks or hymnals and inviting them to join in singing the closing song you have selected.

7. End the session with any last-minute announcements. Refreshments may be served at this time.

6 Planning and Strategy
Ready to Begin: Planning Skills

Overview

This chapter, though seemingly consistent in format with those preceding it, will require the three sessions to be done sequentially, in the order they are presented in this chapter. The first session focuses on the development of planning skills and gives the participants the opportunity to put those skills into practice. The second session relies on the planning skills presented and practiced in the first session to enable the participants to develop a plan for an actual activity. Finally, the third session provides for the implementation and evaluation of the event.

Planning plays an important role in leadership because it provides a direction for everyone, even if only one person is involved in the effort. Where groups are concerned, planning allows for the involvement of others—their ideas, gifts, and talents. Having a plan allows progress to be made. This session will introduce basic planning elements and skills to the participants.

Preparation

- Gather the following items:
  - ☐ two or three wooden 2-by-4 or 4-by-4 planks of equal length, preferably 10 feet long
  - ☐ six to nine cement blocks, three for each plank
  - ☐ four tables
  - ☐ several pieces of paper and a pen for each participant
  - ☐ newsprint and markers
- Elevate each plank on three cement blocks. Turn the cement blocks vertically, to create a little height, and place one at each end, allowing the plank to overhang by a couple of inches. Place one block in the middle of the plank to provide some stability.
- Ask for the assistance of at least four adults to help in all three sessions, from the presentation of planning skills to seeing the task through to the end of the event. Be sure to meet with these adults before the session to prepare them for it.

1. Begin the session by gathering the participants and separating them into two teams. For groups of fewer than fifteen, remain as one group. Use your best judgment as to how many participants will fit "snuggly" on each plank. If need be, add another plank and form a third group. Now explain the rules in this way:
  - Look at the elevated planks for a moment. Each team will soon stand on a plank, where the task is to put yourselves in chronological order according to your birthdays without anyone falling off—but there's a catch. Although you will be able to talk during the activity, you will not be able to say the names of months or numbers.

- Be creative in thinking how you could describe your birth month, as well as the day. As of right now, your team has 60 seconds to talk through and plan a strategy.

2. Ask the adult leaders to help mix up the individuals of the teams, in case some of them have thought of standing near someone whose birthday they know. Now have the teams carefully get onto and stand on the planks. Tell them that you will give them a signal to start. Remind them that if anyone falls off, the team must return to its original order and start again. When ready, give the signal to start.

3. Following the activity, invite the participants to sit together; then initiate a large-group discussion by asking the following questions:
- What was your team's plan? How was it carried out?
- How does planning make a difference in an activity like this one?
- What are the benefits of having a plan?
- How is having a plan helpful in leadership?

4. Now make the following points in these or similar words:
- Planning plays an important role in leadership because it provides a direction for everyone.
- Where groups are concerned, planning allows for the involvement of others, their ideas, gifts, and talents. Having a plan allows for progress to be made.
- A good leader has a plan. Jesus had one.
- We see this with Jesus in the Scriptures. His plan was to spread God's love to the Israelites, even if it meant death on a cross. That, you might say, was his goal.
- Jesus also had many objectives. "How" he spread God's love included gathering a group of friends, or Apostles, with whom he could relate, build relationships, trust, and reveal himself in profound ways.
- Jesus gave these special followers clear goals and objectives regarding how they could carry on the faith and continue his mission on earth.

5. Separate the participants into four equally sized "teams" at four tables. At least one adult should work with each team. Present to the participants the planning elements of goals, objectives, and strategies as noted below:
- A goal is something one strives to accomplish or achieve. It is the "what." An example of a goal is, *to make the team next season.*
- An objective is the "how" of attaining the goal. A few examples for the goal of making the team next season are *to develop a workout schedule, to remain faithful to the workout schedule, to seek pointers from the coach.*
- Each objective may have more detailed objectives that relate and further outline how to attain the goal. For example, with the objective *to develop a workout schedule*, a sub-objective would be *to use weights twice a week or to run two miles every other day.*
- A strategy takes the details even further by determining dates, times, and the people who are responsible. It asks the remaining "who, when, and where." To continue with our example, a strategy for *to use weights twice a week* would be *I will focus on working my upper body on Tuesdays and my lower body on Thursdays of each week, beginning the first week of July and ending the last week of August.*

Following the discussion, ask the participants the following questions:
- How might these elements be helpful in planning various events and activities, whether at school—for example, your sports teams and clubs—in the parish, or within the local community?
- How might goals, objectives, and strategies help you in your own life?

6. Distribute a few pieces of paper and a pen to each participant, and provide them with the following directions:
- For this next activity, you will be working alone.
- Let's pretend that each of you has been given one free day to do with as you wish, and awarded two hundred dollars to spend by the end of that day.
- Your task is to write out a plan for yourself, determining a goal, some objectives, and some strategies of how you will spend your day and the money. When finished, you will have the opportunity to share your plan with your small group.

After 10 minutes call the small groups together for the participants to share their plans. Ask for a volunteer from each group to share that group's plan with the larger group.

7. Now present the roles of facilitator and note taker in this way:
- Another important element in planning are the roles of the facilitator and the note taker.
- The facilitator is the person who manages the flow of discussion of a group. She or he is responsible for involving everyone in the discussion, as well as managing the discussion well so that no one member dominates the group or the ideas and opinions of a member go unheard.
- For our next activity, the adult leaders of your teams will help the person who will serve in the facilitator role.
- The role of the note taker is equally important; he or she is responsible for noting the opinions and ideas of the group by writing them down and keeping a record of them.
- For our activity, this will be done on the newsprint provided to your group. You will need to recruit one participant from your group to serve as the facilitator and one as the note taker.

8. In these or similar words, present the small groups with the following task:
- Let's pretend that each of the small groups in this room have just been awarded $10,000 to spend as they wish.
- Take about 20 minutes to work together to determine a goal, some objectives, and some strategies for how you will use that money.

When finished, ask each of the small groups to present their goal, objectives, and strategies to the large group. Point out when the groups have appropriately developed these elements, according to your outline. Make any corrections needed.

9. Wrap up the session by sharing the following points:
- The most important reason for a plan is that it helps us live out a clear mission. Once we have a purpose, we're ready to set the ball in motion to accomplish our goals.

- This is what Jesus did. He grew to know his mission through prayer, his connection with God the Father. Once he knew his mission—to share God's love by serving the poor in various ways—he was then able to move forward with it and live it. With a mission and a plan, we have a clear direction.
- The Christian leader who is rooted and shares in the mission of Jesus is called to continue in that mission. How we do that—our plan—is determined by the resources available to us, including the gifts, talents, and creativity each of us has been given by God to use accordingly.

10. Make any final announcements, including the next meeting time and location.

Ready to Be Formed: Planning Skills in Practice

Overview

The most important reason for a plan is that it helps us live out a clear mission. Once we have a purpose, we're ready to set the ball in motion to accomplish our goals. This session capitalizes on the planning skills learned in the first session, so be sure you have conducted the first session before implementing this one. The participants will develop objectives, strategies, tasks, and various other elements to implement an event that will occur during the third session.

Preparation

- Gather the following items:
  - ☐ newsprint and markers
  - ☐ 3-by-5-inch index cards, one for each participant
- On each index card, write down one portion of an ingredient, as outlined below, and continue to do so until all portions of the ingredients have been written on an index card. For example, on one index card write the following: 2 large cloves of garlic placed in a plastic bag. The ingredients below are divided equally for a group of twenty-five participants. For larger groups of participants, multiply the ingredients accordingly:
  - ☐ nine index cards on which is written: one package of twelve dinner rolls
  - ☐ two index cards on which is written: two tablespoons olive oil placed in an airtight plastic bag
  - ☐ four index cards on which is written: two 16-ounce cans of chicken broth
  - ☐ two index cards on which is written: two large cloves of garlic placed in a plastic bag
  - ☐ two index cards on which is written: three large yellow onions
  - ☐ two index cards on which is written: three large potatoes
  - ☐ two index cards on which is written: two 16-ounce cans of diced tomatoes
  - ☐ one index card on which is written: one bag of fresh spinach
  - ☐ one index card on which is written: one tablespoon salt and one tablespoon pepper; one tablespoon oregano or basil placed in an airtight plastic bag (optional)

1. Gather the participants and begin the session by asking the following questions for review:
  - What is a goal? Can anyone give an example of a goal?
  - What is an objective? Can anyone give some examples of objectives for the goal mentioned?
  - What is a strategy? What would be some strategies to use with the objectives just mentioned?

Now briefly review the following from the previous session:
  - A goal is something one strives to accomplish or achieve. It is the "what."
  - An objective is the "how" of attaining the goal.

- Each objective may have more detailed objectives that relate to and further outline how to attain the goal.
- A strategy takes the details even further by determining dates, times, and the people who are responsible. It asks the remaining "who, when, and where."

2. Announce to the participants that they will be developing a plan for a simple supper, which will involve making soup. In large-group discussion, determine a purpose for the activity, for example, to supply the parish community, to donate to a local soup kitchen, and so on. Record what is brainstormed on newsprint.

3. Divide the participants into small groups of five or six people. Distribute some markers and one sheet of newsprint to each small group. Invite the groups to work with the goal by developing some possible objectives to be shared with the large group to help determine the plan. The following is an example of what you might start to develop:
- Purpose ("why" you want to accomplish the goal): To offer young people of the parish an opportunity to serve others during the season of Lent
- Goal ("what" you want to accomplish): To plan and implement a simple supper
- Objectives ("how" you will accomplish the goal):
  + by serving the parish community
  + by inviting more young people to become involved in the event
  + by publicizing the event
  + by forming different teams to oversee the various tasks involved

After 15 minutes, encourage the teams to finish up and prepare to present to the large group their ideas, which will serve as objectives for the plan.

4. In the large-group setting, together organize and determine the objectives for the plan from those presented. Point out that the objectives generated for the goal could serve as the tasks of the various teams to be formed. For example, if the objective is to publicize the event, a publicity team could be formed. Chopping and cooking are another task, so a cooking team could be formed. Now identify and organize the different tasks to be performed according to category, such as cooking, set up and decorating, serving stations, and so on. Once identified, ask each group to volunteer to oversee and determine strategies for the tasks within the category they have taken on. The following are examples of possible strategies for the objectives offered above:
- Strategies (answering the questions of who, when, and where):
  + The event could be held in the church hall on the third Friday of Lent, following the stations of the cross.
  + Each young person involved in the planning will personally invite another young person to be involved in the event. If the invitation is accepted, the person involved in the planning will ask the person they've invited to bring half of what they have been assigned to bring as an ingredient for the soup.
  + A small team of three or four people will work with Mr. Smith to write up an ad for the Sunday bulletin and to create twenty posters to post around town.
  + The various tasks involved include setting up the tables and decorating the room where the dinner will be served; preparing the table linens, dinnerware, paper goods, and beverage station; chopping and cooking; clean up;

and developing or acquiring a meal prayer in which to lead everyone before the meal. Either each small group will take on these tasks or teams will be formed.

5. Ask the participants to once again gather in their small groups. Provide each group with another sheet of newsprint to develop a list of strategies they will use to accomplish their assigned tasks. Allow the teams to work for approximately 20 minutes.

6. Gather the small groups for large-group sharing and discussion, making sure the plan is clear and well thought out. Offer any questions to the group appropriate to any tasks needing further development.

7. Now do a final check with the teams to make sure everything is accounted for and part of the plan. Ask the participants what they're thinking and how they're feeling about the event at this point and the tasks before them. Remind them of these effects:
- This event is not merely "something nice to do."
- Serving in this way connects them more deeply to the mission and to the person of Jesus, not only by the offering of soup to the hungry at a local soup kitchen or by serving others in the name of Jesus, but by leading other Catholics into a deeper sense of prayer and fasting, thus providing an opportunity to stand in solidarity with one another, whether through presence, through prayer, or by meeting another's need.
- Their leadership through this effort continues to proclaim the Good News of God's love.

8. At this time, randomly distribute the index cards, one to each of the participants. Inform them that they are to bring the exact amount described on the card, as each ingredient is vital to the outcome of the soup. Be sure everyone understands what they are to do, and make the following connection:
- As each of us has been given the resources, gifts, talents, and creativity to share with others, God depends on each of us to truly be the Body of Christ in the world. The creation of our pot of soup will depend on what each of us has to offer. If one ingredient is missing, the soup suffers; it is less than what it could be.
- Please remember to bring the portion of the ingredient listed on the index card that has been given to you—no more and no less than what is listed. Each of you is needed for the soup to be all that it can be.

9. Make any final announcements, including the next meeting time and location. You may also choose to conduct the closing prayer service, "Prayer of Sending Forth, at the end of this chapter.

Never Too Young to Lead

Ready to Be Empowered: Implementing the Plan

Overview

We are called to be leaders not for ourselves or our own gain, but for the benefit of others. We must remember that through us God works, and that is what Christian leadership is all about. This session capitalizes on the planning skills learned in the first session as well as the plan developed in the second session, so be sure you have conducted the first and second session before implementing this one.

Note: As the preparation on the day of the event, as well as the event itself, will demand more time than the normal time allotted for a session, please plan accordingly. This session, like the previous one, is planned based on a group of twenty-five participants.

Preparation

- Gather the following items:
  - ☐ newsprint
  - ☐ nametags and thin-line markers
  - ☐ food items to be brought by the young people: dinner rolls, cloves of garlic, bags of fresh spinach, cans of diced tomatoes, potatoes, and onions, separated according to the recipe, for approximately 100 people
  - ☐ food items to be purchased, as outlined in the recipe, as well as butter or margarine for the dinner rolls, coffee, tea, sugar, cream, bottled water, and ice, for approximately 100 people
  - ☐ paper items: napkins, coffee cups, cold cups, plastic dinnerware, and soup bowls for approximately 100 people
  - ☐ salt and pepper packets or shakers for each table
  - ☐ coordinated decorative items for the dining space: table decorations, table linens, serving dishes, and so on
  - ☐ aprons, chopping knives, and serving spoons; each participant to bring for their own use
  - ☐ three or four crock pots for the serving area, with ladles
  - ☐ two large pots for the soup, size determined by the quantity to be made
  - ☐ *Stone Soup*, by Marcia Brown (New York: Simon and Schuster Children's Publishing Division, 1975), checked out from the local library or purchased at a local bookstore
  - ☐ newsprint
  - ☐ copies of handout 4, "A Simple Recipe for Soup," for each participant
- Make the necessary preparations to reserve the parish kitchen facility or another kitchen facility to prepare the meal.
- If the meal is intended to be for the parish community, ensure that proper publicity has been distributed and invitations have been extended. If the meal is to be brought to a local homeless shelter, ensure that the proper arrangements have been made.

- A day or so before the gathering, you will want to provide the young people with a reminder regarding their "assigned" ingredient. You can do that via e-mail or by phone.

1. As the participants arrive, invite each person to print his or her name on a nametag and to wear it in a visible area.

2. Ask the participants to place their food items and cooking utensils in the kitchen, and then gather the group, seating them together, to set the tone for the event through the use of a story.

3. Read *Stone Soup*, by Marcia Brown, a story that illustrates how a community benefits from sharing what each person has to offer, whether it be their gifts, talents, personalities, or possessions. When finished, ask the following questions during a brief, large-group sharing:
   - What about the story makes an impression on you?
   - What does this story have to teach us about what we are doing today?

4. Now make the following points in these or your own words:
   - We have taken the time to prepare and put into action a plan for this event, not for our own need but for the need of others. We have been called by God to use the blessings we've been given for the good of others.
   - We are called to be leaders, not for ourselves or our own gain but for the benefit of others. We must remember that through us, God works, and that is what Christian leadership is all about.
   - The story *Stone Soup* illustrates our need for community and the need the community has for our participation, whether it be our presence or our action—or both. Today we are God's instruments in being of service to others.
   - Let's remember that the most important reason for a plan is that it helps us live out a clear mission. Once we have a purpose, we're ready to set the ball in motion toward accomplishing our goals.
   - This is what Jesus did. He grew to know his mission through prayer, his connection with God the Father. Once he knew his mission—to share God's love by serving the poor in various ways—he was then able to move forward with it and live it. With a mission and a plan, we have a clear direction.
   - That is what we are doing today. We are rooted in and share in the mission of Jesus, and we continue his mission through serving others in his name today.
   - Our plan was determined by the resources available to us, including the gifts, talents, and creativity each of us has been given by God to use accordingly. Our plan is allowing us to live the mission of Jesus today.

5. Ask the group to join you in prayer as you begin this time of service, by praying together in the words Jesus taught: *Our Father . . .*

6. Now separate the participants into teams according to the outlined tasks. Distribute copies of handout 4 to those preparing the soup. Begin preparations; then conduct the actual serving and supper.

7. Following the event, gather the group to conduct an evaluation of the event and the planning process. Separate the participants into groups of five or six that are different from the teams that worked together on the tasks. Provide one piece of newsprint for each group to record their findings and evaluations. The following are some questions to use to assess the event:
- What has been the feedback from the event? What specific aspects of the event were commented on?
- How well did we accomplish our goal?
- On a scale of 1 to 10, with 10 being excellent and 1 being poor, where on the scale did we fall in terms of developing the plan? (Average out the numerical responses of all group members. Discuss why each person chose the number she or he did as well as what contributed to making the plan strong or weak.)
- Where on the scale did we fall in terms of teamwork? (Average out each person's numerical response. Discuss why each person chose the number she or he did, as well as what contributed to strong or weak teamwork.)
- How did missing group members (and ingredients) affect the soup (and the event)? Why is it important that all key elements (and people) be included in a plan?
- What were some of the leadership skills used during the planning process and implementation of the event?
- What were some of the different gifts shared by individuals of the group? How did these support the group's effort? How would things have played out differently if some of the gifts were not shared?
- How did having a plan make this event possible? What specifically did the plan help us do and accomplish?
- What was the best part of the process for you? Was there a part of the process that you were challenged by or struggled with? Why?
- What did you learn about leadership through this entire process? How will what you learned help you in the future when working with groups or planning on your own?
- How was the mission of Jesus carried out through our plan and our efforts? What difference has this made for others? What difference has this made for us?

Invite the small groups to share their discussions with the large group.

Prayer of Sending Forth

Preparation

- Gather the following items:
    - ☐ parish hymnals or worship aids
    - ☐ *The Catholic Youth Bible* or another Bible
- Select a song that complements the Scripture reading, such as "What You Have Done," by Tony Alonso (*Gather Comprehensive,* third edition, GIA Publications).
- Invite some of the young people to lead the song selected, either vocally or instrumentally, to conclude the prayer.
- Invite one young person to proclaim Matthew 25:34–40. Prepare the young person by reviewing the passage together beforehand.

1. Invite the group to join you in a space for prayer, all standing in one large circle. Ask the group to quiet their bodies, minds, and hearts to recognize God's presence within and around them.

2. Begin by inviting the participants to bless themselves with the sign of the cross as you say: "In the name of the Father, and of the Son, and of the Holy Spirit. Amen." Then offer the following prayer:
- Lord, we come before you as leaders called to live by the example of Jesus: to be seekers of justice, to love tenderly, and to walk humbly with you, our God (adapted from Mic. 6:8).
- Help us to be reminded of this call whenever we are faced with the very real reminders of the injustices of this world. Teach us to respond to them by using the gifts you have given us, in the ordinary ways that we can.
- Unite us to you so that we may become creators, builders, and restorers of the world you created for us.
- We ask all this in the name of Jesus Christ, our Lord. Amen.

3. Invite the participants to prepare their hearts to listen to God's word through the Scripture reading from Matthew's Gospel. Then invite the prepared young person to proclaim Matthew 25:34–40. Follow with a brief moment of silence. In response to the Gospel proclamation, invite the participants to sing together a few verses of the song you have selected.

4. Ask the group to join hands and participate in a "squeeze prayer," providing them with the following directions:
- I will begin the prayer, and every person has the option of either mentioning an intention for what or whom they would like to pray, or pausing to pray in silence.
- When I am finished with my prayer, I will squeeze the hand of the person to my left. That person can then pray aloud or pause and pray silently.
- When you have finished your prayer, squeeze the hand of the person to your left. This action will continue until everyone in the circle has been given the opportunity to pray. (Be sure everyone understands before you begin.)

5. When everyone has had an opportunity to pray, conclude by offering the following prayer:
- Lord, we are confident that you hear our prayers, and we look to your help and guidance in making our world a better place.
- Help us to choose our styles of leadership wisely, so that we may be true examples of your compassion, forgiveness, and love for the people we meet.
- We ask this through Christ, our Lord. Amen.

Let us conclude our prayer in thanksgiving to God as we say, *"Glory be to the Father . . ."*

6. End the session with any last-minute announcements.

A Simple Recipe for Soup

The following recipe is simple, quick to make and easy to adjust according to your need. It is traditionally known as Italian Flag Soup, as the colors of the ingredients are those of the Italian flag. It is meatless, though a favorite meat could easily be added if so desired. The recipe below is designed to make one large, industrial-sized pot of soup, to feed approximately 100 people. Adjust accordingly for a larger or smaller anticipated crowd.

- nine packages of dinner rolls (twelve per package)
- four tablespoons olive oil
- six large yellow onions, chopped
- four large cloves of garlic, minced
- eight 16-ounce cans of chicken broth
- six large potatoes, peeled, cut in two, and sliced approximately one-fourth inch thick
- four 16-ounce cans of diced tomatoes
- one tablespoon salt and one tablespoon pepper; oregano or basil is optional
- one bag of fresh spinach, chopped

In a large, industrial-sized pot, combine olive oil, onions, and garlic, and cook until onions are softened and translucent, stirring constantly. Add chicken broth and potatoes and bring to a boil, stirring occasionally. Let boil for 10 minutes, lower the heat, and add tomatoes, salt, and pepper, along with any additional spices if so desired. Finally, add the spinach 10 minutes before serving and stir into the soup.

Handout 4: Permission to reproduce is granted. © 2006 by Saint Mary's Press.

Acknowledgments

The scriptural quotations contained herein are from the New Revised Standard Version of the Bible, Catholic Edition. Copyright © 1993 and 1989 by the Division of Christian Education of the National Council of the Churches of Christ in the United States of America. All rights reserved.

Portions of the activity "How We Approach Conflict" on pages 39–41 and handout 2 are adapted from *Dealing with Tough Times,* by Marilyn Kielbasa (Winona, MN: Saint Mary's Press, 1999), page 52; and *Dealing with Tough Times* student workbook, pages 16–19. Copyright © 1999 by Saint Mary's Press. All rights reserved.

The mediation session on pages 42–43 is based on the activity "Car Auction," in *Warm-ups for Meeting Leaders,* by Sue Bianchi, Jan Butler, and David Richey (Ventura, CA: Quality Group Publishing, 1984), page 107. Copyright © 1984 by Quality Group Publishing.

The five-step process of mediating on pages 43–44 and handout 3 is adapted from *Mediation: Getting to WinWin!* teacher's guide, by Fran Schmidt (Miami: Peace Education Foundation, 1994), pages 28–29. Copyright © 1994 by Grace Contrino Abrams Peace Education Foundation.

During this book's preparation, all citations, facts, figures, names, addresses, telephone numbers, Internet URLs, and other pieces of information cited within were verified for accuracy. The authors and Saint Mary's Press staff have made every attempt to reference current and valid sources, but we cannot guarantee the content of any source, and we are not responsible for any changes that may have occurred since our verification. If you find an error in, or have a question or concern about, any of the information or sources listed within, please contact Saint Mary's Press.